AF572063

Many, many, many thanks to:

David Larson Productions
5910 North Lilly Road
Menomonee Falls, Wisconsin 53051

Producers:	Dave and Kate Larson
Director:	Ivy Revolinski
Editor:	Pete Pfankuch
Engineer:	John Kraft
Stylist:	Luella Doss
Production:	Jeff Cartier, Mike Geracci, David C. Larson, Dan Quinn, Tom Reardon, Mark Schwerin, Andy Steiber
Models:	Luella Doss, Debbie Kraft, Jennifer Larson, Maribel Steiber, and Kathy Thompson

And to Rebecca Feehan Adams for her publishing expertise

A grateful acknowledgment to these quality companies for partial underwriting of the television series:

New Home/Janome Sewing Machine Company
100 Hollister Road
Teterboro, NJ 07608
(201) 440-8080
Delightful machines with which you can make it special

Bonfit America
5959 Triumph Street
Commerce, CA 90040-1688
(800) 342-9555
The adjustable patterners for all sizes, all styles

Coats and Clark
30 Patewood Drive, Suite 351
Greenville, SC 29612
(803) 234-0331
Providing threads and notions to accommodate your every sewing need

Donna Salyers Fabulous Furs and FabuLeather
700 Madison Avenue
Covington, KY 41011
(606) 291-3300
Beautiful faux furs and leathers easy to sew and care for

The Sewing Connection
Series 11

Shirley Adams Publications
• 922 Cheltenham Way • Plainfield, IN 46168 •
1-800-237-4475

Available from Shirley Adams Publications
- ***The Sewing Connection*** books and accompanying videos *
- **Belt Bazaar Video** ~ a trunk show of hundreds of unique belts you can make that serve functional to decorative. Each belt is made from one simple pattern that is included with the purchase of the book. These belts are made by incorporating no-sew fusible web.
- **Belt Bazaar book** ~ a workbook designed to show you how to sew hundreds of belts using fabrics that match your outfit and making fasteners out of trinkets.
- **Celebration of Jackets Video** ~ a trunk show of beautiful, elegant and functional jackets lined and single layer that you create with changes to one basic pattern. No one but you knows the secret!
- **Blouse Pattern Pizazz** book and video ~ learn how to make dozens of different blouses from just 1 simple pattern. How to make those sought after no-pattern blouses, coats. Learn designer secrets of making flattering tops to fit any figure.

* Each video series and accompanying workbook contain the 13 segments you watch on public television. Each cover beginning to advanced sewing techniques. Always new and always innovative, Shirley shows you how to be the professional designer – from changing patterns to creating them. As Shirley says, "Homemade is only good when it comes from the kitchen!" Video series available in sets only, but all books can stand independently of the videos.

Printed in the United States of America

The Sewing Connection Series 11

Chameleon Wardrobing Program 1

Welcome to series 11 of ***The Sewing Connection***. Sewers are my favorite people and I get a lot of mail saying thanks for the inspiration. But you also inspire me. When I'm on my frequent travels presenting live seminars I see wonderful ideas that start my wheels turning.

Out west in a fashion show was a chameleon vest I thought ingenious. One simple piece opens up flat. Two of these pieces button back and front to make a vest. Finish each side of these two in different fabrics and embellishments, and they become four sides to switch about in every conceivable way. Button the points together or have the flat edges side by side. Mix it so a point and a flat are joined together complicating it further by buttoning it either toward the left or the right. There are buttonholes in both edges. The buttons are separate from the vest, two joined by a shank like cuff links. A vest needs three sets each in front and back for a total of twelve buttons.

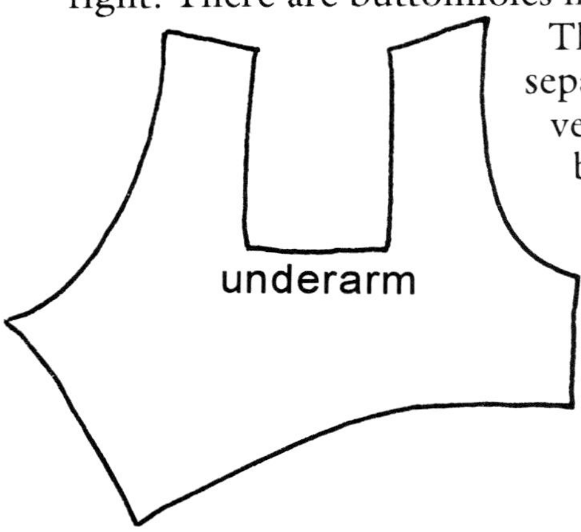

Fabric Choice

Karen Odam of Dos de Tejas (two Texans) was the clever lady behind all this. Think wisely about what your four sides will be. The vest can act as a catalyst to blend a closet full of garments.

I started my vest with three colors in mind because I noticed them together in several prints. My thinking was to mix them with solids for endless possibilities. Purple, turquoise and cinnamon may not seem too likely, but a pant outfit in a solid color of each will make great background for each of the vest mixes.

Playing with fabric combinations is such fun that it is difficult to stop with one vest so I made two. Only time limitations prevented doing several more. I found, looking through my stash that the perfect combinations go on forever.

Thinking your way through, deciding which fabrics should back each other, is the hardest part of the whole project. Here's how those decisions work:

Two polished cotton upholstery fabrics are coordinates. The prints have identical colors but are in contrasting scales, large and small. These would obviously be good worn together, so should be used on two different halves.

Two others, a stylized paisley and a leafy natural print do not blend. Some of the colors are similar but most are not. One is a crisp closely woven polished cotton with a metallic filigree overprint, a festive feeling. The other is a loosely woven soft challis. The mood is just too different to be worn together. These two opposites would therefore do very well stitched back to back. Each side could then be paired with several other possibilities but never with each other.

This would then be how to plan: back-to-back if they never would mix, on separate vest parts if they blend attractively. You can see this needs careful thinking to make each side work with every other possibility.

The Dos de Tejas pattern is multi-sized including everything from 8 up to 18. Fit closely in the bust it hangs straight to the waist with no shape. Trace this in your size from the Dos de Tejas pattern on another sheet of paper or some fibrous pattern tracer.

Mounting Fabrics

Depending on the fabric chosen and the weight of embellishments added, it may be wise to mount the fashion fabric on a backing of some sort. If this section needs some "beefing up," consider a firm cotton or polyester batting. This is sometimes called clothing fleece and is sold by the yard in the interfacing department or in pre-measured lengths in a package. Cotton flannel might be another alternative, lighter in weight. Be sure to pre-shrink this by washing in hot water before cutting out. Still lighter weight but lending some stability might be cotton batiste. A fusible interfacing is yet another alternative. You be the judge as to what is appropriate.

Stitch any of these to the back side of the fashion fabric before adding trims for decorative stitching. Some fabrics will need no backing.

In some cases only one heavy fabric might be used, each side having a different look. Such was the case with a vest shown which belonged to the designer. One vest section was leather, smooth on one side. The reverse side was merely the rougher suede side. Another heavy fabric Karen Odam used was covered with shaggy strings, the reverse side smooth.

Left-Right Reminder

If more than one layer will be stitched together, the outline shapes must be pointed properly in order that the fabric wrong sides will be back-to-back. Cut in the wrong direction, the layer will be unusable. I found it easiest to pin a little scrap of the fabrics to be used on each pattern side. This clearly showed which way to cut, preventing mistakes.

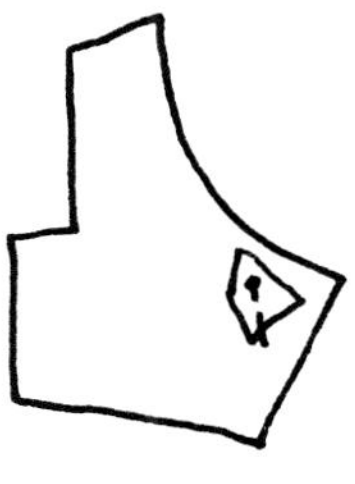

Edging

If these layers will be UltraSuede® (as one of my vest parts is) the simplest finish is to merely edge-stitch the layers together in several parallel rows. This will only work for heavy duty suedes. The lighter varieties of synthetic suedes and leathers would require either a seam all around the edge or a binding to make that edge heavier and firmer. Make that binding of any fabric, knit or woven. It works well in animal or man-made suede or leather. Purchased fold-over braid would be another option. This edging is all part of the fun putting together the fabrics, trims, buttons that belong; that make it exciting; that make you love to sew!

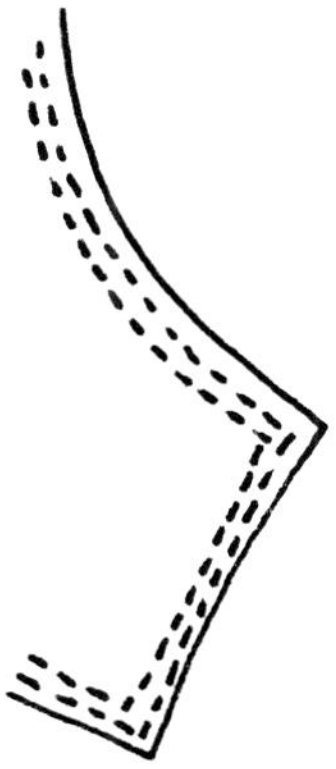

Bias Binding

Cut woven fabric on a 45° angle bias. The strips should begin about 2" wide. When pulled through a 1" wide metal bias tape maker, the edges will fold over uniformly to make a perfect binding.

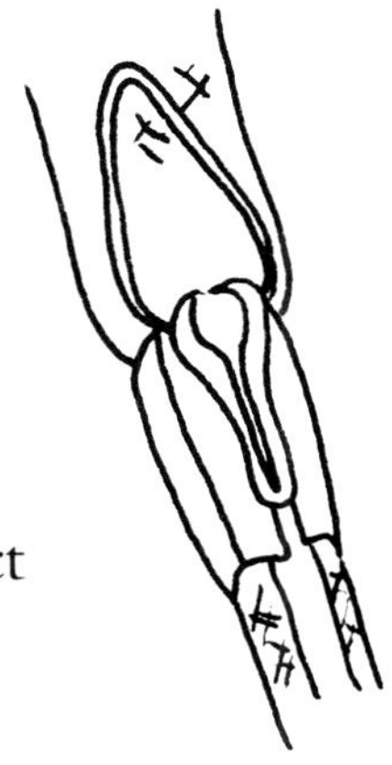

Several strips of this must be joined either before cutting bias (continuous bias) or after the strips have been cut. If these are joined afterwards be very sure to cut the edges to be joined **on grain** rather than straight across. To cut and stitch across the bias in this manner would undoubtedly stretch and ripple somewhat making it less than attractive. A secondary reason is that this would put all the bulk in the same location. Joining this on the fabric straight grain results in not only a nearly invisible flat seam, but also distributes the seam bulk so that it is barely noticeable.

not this

To attach this binding one choice could be one-step topstitching. Fold the tape (edges already pressed in) in half again ... or nearly so. You actually want the underside slightly wider so that when you topstitch from the top side, the underside will also be caught in the stitching. This can stiffen the edge considerably so may not be desirable. Another drawback may be that the stitching shows.

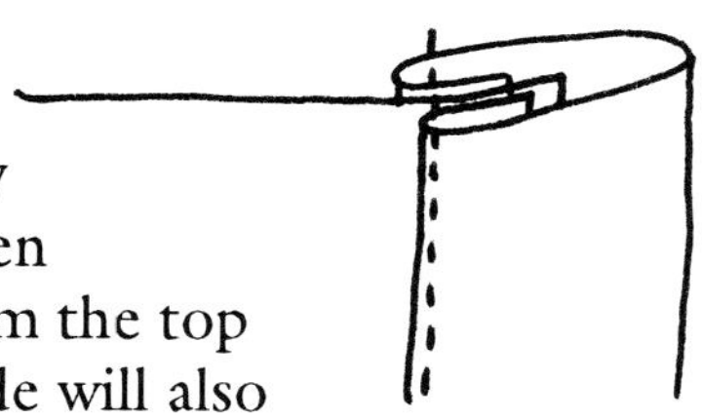

The more usual way may be a two-step method where you stitch only the tape seam allowance to the garment for the first step. Fold then to the back side making sure that its back folded edge slightly covers the original stitching line. Stitch in the ditch — the line where the binding and fabric connect. It will not show on the front, but stitches will be close to folded edge on the backside. This often looks better and is softer when completed.

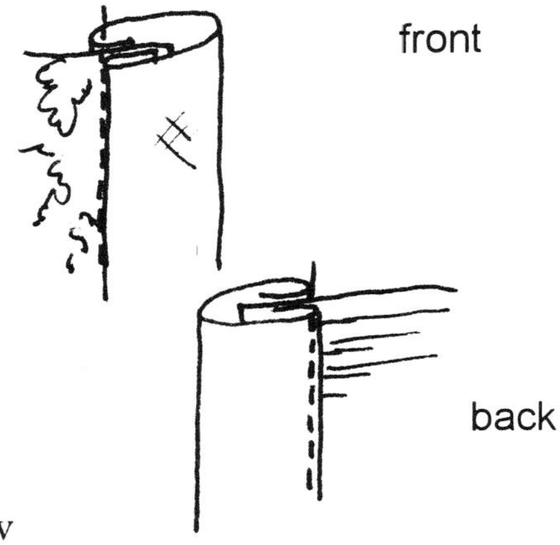

Consider also what will happen at the corners. Because there will be inside and outside corners, mitering both might look best. With the outside corner, remember that the extreme outer corner will be larger than the stitching line where bias and vest attach. That means extra fabric must be incorporated into the corner by adding a little pleat. A simple way to do this is to stitch the bias to the vest edge, right sides together. When you approach the corner, ***stop a seams' width short***. Pivot slightly, and stitch diagonally out to the corner and off the fabric.

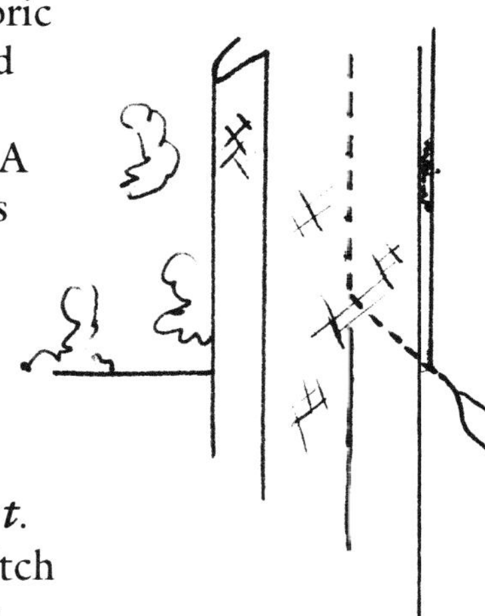

Turn 90º, and fold bias so that it squares the corner. A fold will result overlapping the edge just stitched. The outer

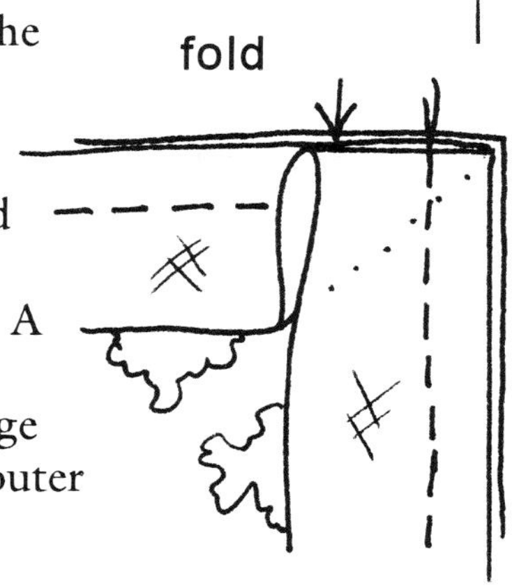

bias edge will be aligned with the new vest side. Start a new line of stitching to attach the new side.

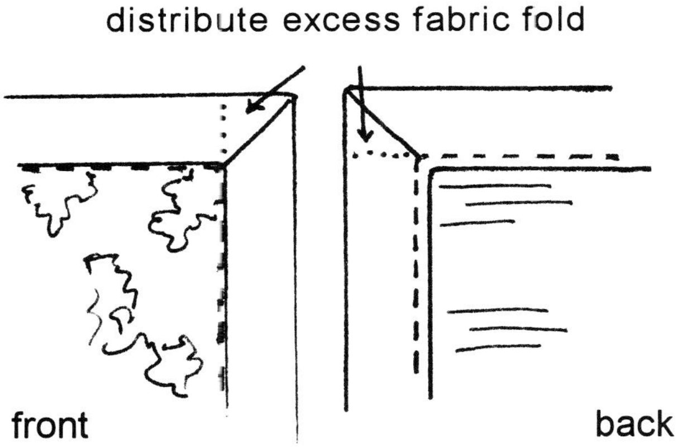

When stitched, open up the bias away from the vest to fold out wider. Then fold part of the bias to the backside so it encloses the raw edge and slightly covers the original stitching line. There will be a triangle of excess fabric in the corner both on front and back sides. Fold them in opposite directions before the final stitching to distribute the bulk between the layers.

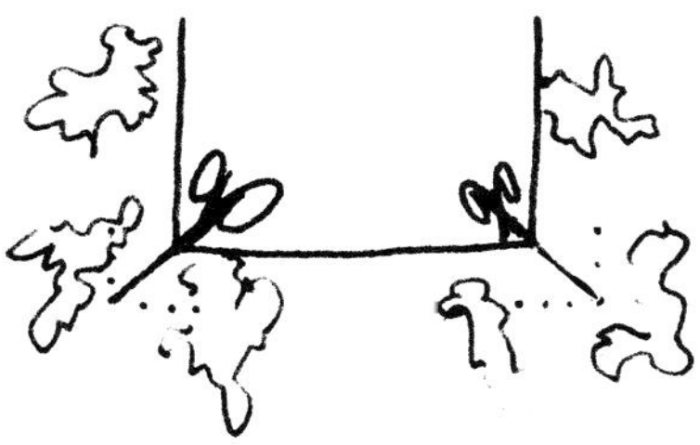

Clip inside corners on the vest up to the planned stitching line. The fabric then opens up into a straight line as it is sewn to the bias binding strip, right sides together. When this inside corner strip is folded in place, extra fabric results at the outside edge which is smaller. Miter excess

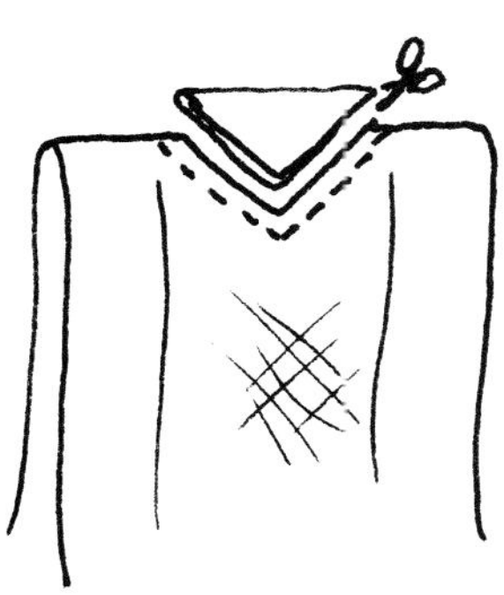

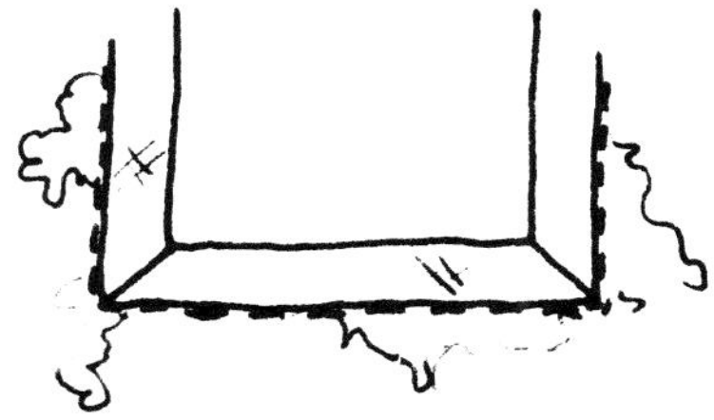

by machine stitching and trimming out at each inside corner on the binding strip. Since this is only a narrow strip and is in underarm areas besides, it is permissible to instead finish off all the machine stitching in a straight line. Let the project straighten in a flat position at which time the binding ripples in the corners. Fold it into a miter and hand tack the very corner into place.

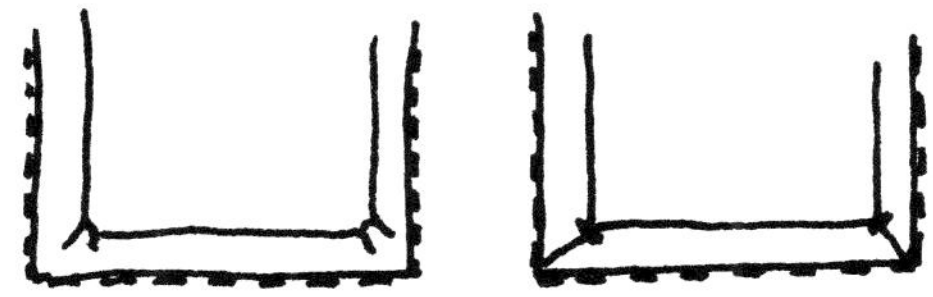

A suede strip binding needs no seam allowances Just cut it the 1" width or whatever size is your preference. Back it with a strip of Wonder Under® or Heat and Bond® – a paper backed fusible web. Peel off the paper backing. Fold almost in half but slightly longer on the underside. Stitch close to the fold, adjusting for uniformity as you progress. The vest raw edges are sandwiched in between layers and fused in place. Now stitch through all layers on the open edge. It is also possible to glue stick this in place rather than fusing, or perhaps just pin to hold until it is stitched.

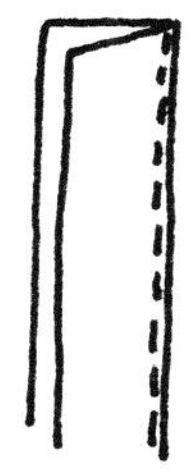

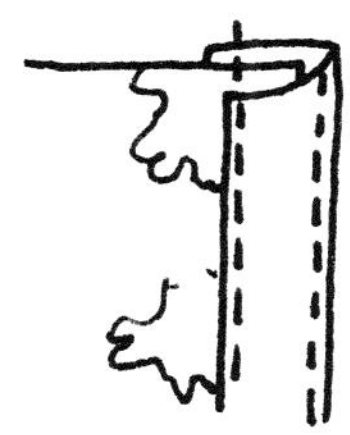

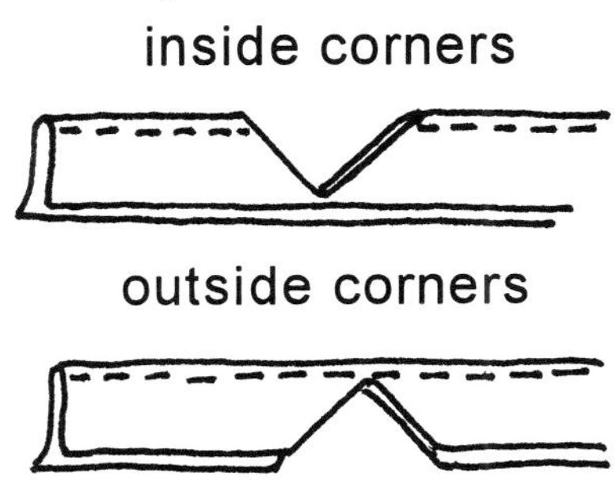

Inside and outside corners can be cut out since raveling is not a problem (above).

Cut these at the same angle as the corner involved before applying the trim.

There is an interesting leather bound buttonhole in this pattern also. Another alternative would, of course, be machine-made buttonholes.

The buttons mentioned are two connected by a thread shank. The outside buttons that show are decorative buttons and probably fairly large so they show up. Choose a small, clear plastic button for the inside because it never shows. The buttonhole need only fit this small button. As illustrated it is stitched together with perhaps a $^1/_2$" shank a few times. Wrap that shank with the same thread length, and a knot catches the end.

This changeable wardrobing idea spawns myriad combinations. Look through your closets and drawers to find other surprises that go together. Spend an afternoon or evening now and then to discover forgotten items that could be useful again. To wear things in different ways gives a whole new perspective and revitalizes your wardrobe.

To order the Dos de Tejas Chameleon Vest pattern
Send $8.95 + $1.50 shipping and handling to
Dos de Tejas • PO Box 1636 • Sherman, TX 75091
or call 1-800-8-Tejas-8 for Mastercard or Visa ordering.

A catalog will come with it showing all the patterns, notions and kits. The buttonhole leather is also available in red, teal, black, tobacco, and taupe. These are fun patterns with a southwest flavor.

Come Fly With Me Program 2

We travel a lot on business and if we fly, I want the window seat. Out that window from way up above, marvelous designs appear if it's cloudless – or at least when taking off and landing. Each city has a flavor all its own, but when I come home the approach to Indianapolis in the spring is what you see on the back cover. Farmers have plowed their fields in contoured lines around hills with only a hint of young crops emerging. The fields are bordered with trees and shrubs leafing out. Everything I see anywhere can easily be reinterpreted in fabrics providing endless inspiration.

When you drive along and look at farmers' fields on the ground, everything looks very straight and squared. But from the air it's a crazy quilt. All the pieces – the "fields" – are odd shapes; they fit together like a puzzle. Let's first make the plowed fields, then fit them on a garment.

Twin needle pintucking is a good way to duplicate the field burrows. The fabric is 100% cotton hand dyed in twelve different gradations of blue ranging from very light to very dark. Those fields may actually be green or brown, but that doesn't mean you can't reinterpret them in blue or red or whatever color pleases you.

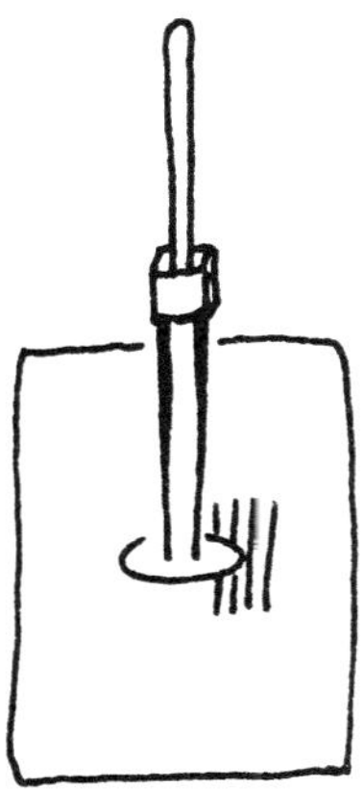

You must use a twin needle, but use any machine that has a large enough throat plate hole so both needles will travel up and down without hitting metal. The needles come in various widths attached to a common shank from about 1.5mm apart up to 4mm. The difference in the tucks after they are stitched is that the wider ones will have a much bigger or higher fold of fabric than the narrow spacing. What causes this is the single bobbin thread pulling the two top threads together forming a fold of fabric between them. I used a 2.5 needle.

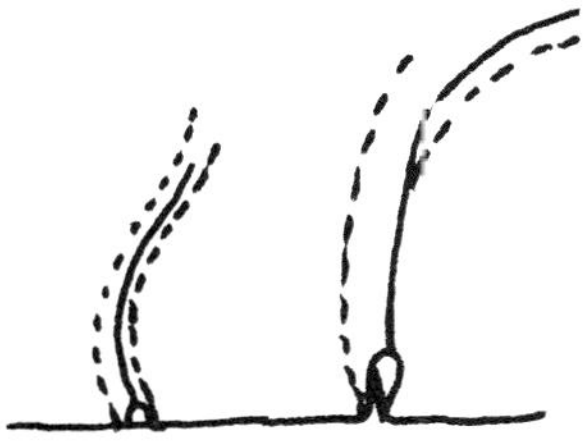

For the two threads you'll need two spool pins or two small spools of thread on one pin. Thread the machine with both threads together until the last thread guide right before the needles. Separate here, one thread through the guide, the other bypassing it and going directly to a needle.

Stitch one row in a curvy line to set a pattern. Stitch several more parallel rows using the edge of the foot as a guide. It is also possible to make these rows closer together by setting the grooved pintuck foot with a groove in the foot overlapping the former stitched row. When all my fabrics were stitched in curvy designs I cut the fabrics into smaller odd-shaped pieces. Incidentally, the curvy rows duplicated the contour plowing of hillsides in southern Indiana.

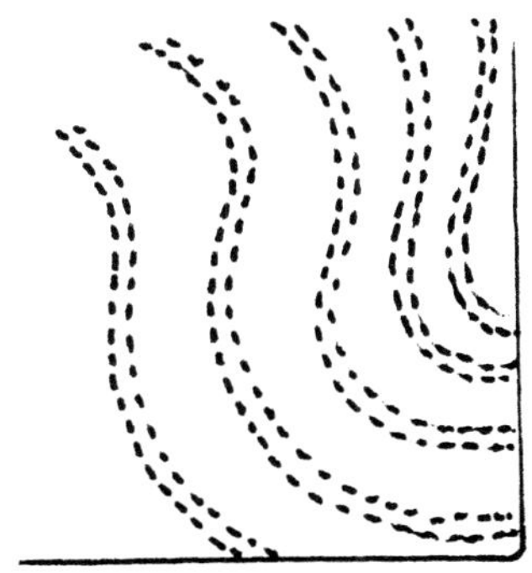

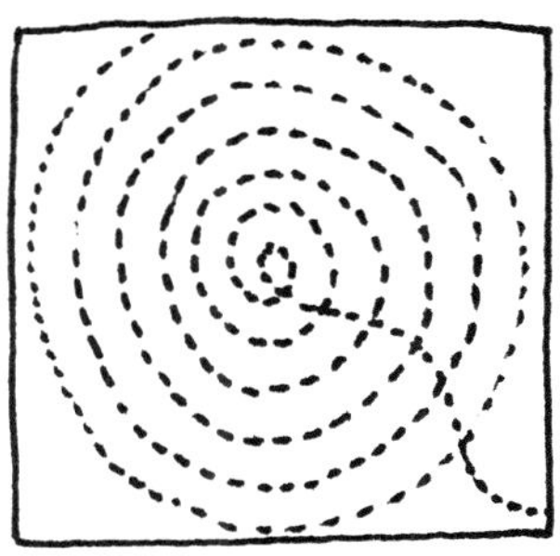

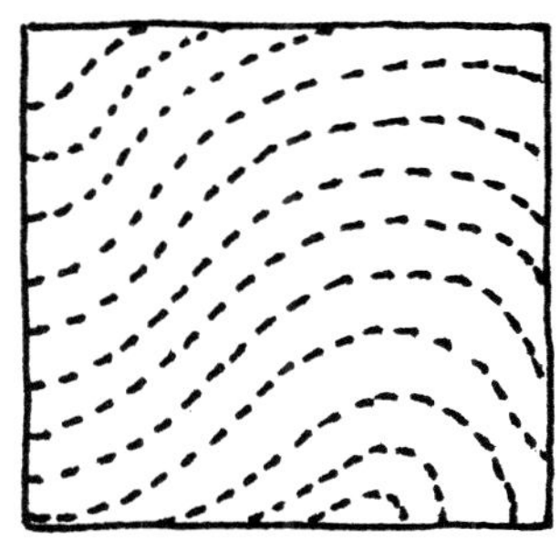

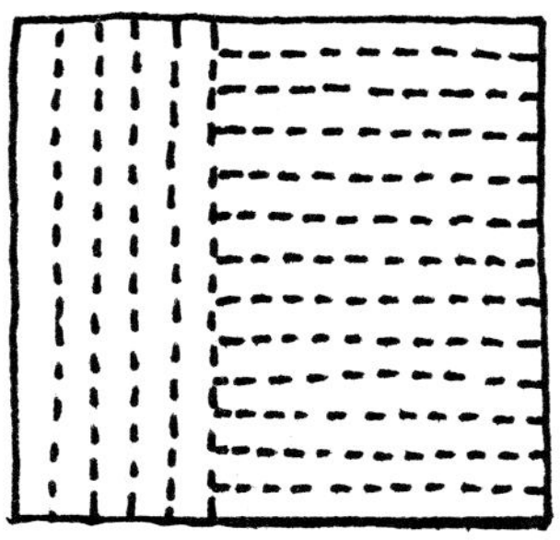

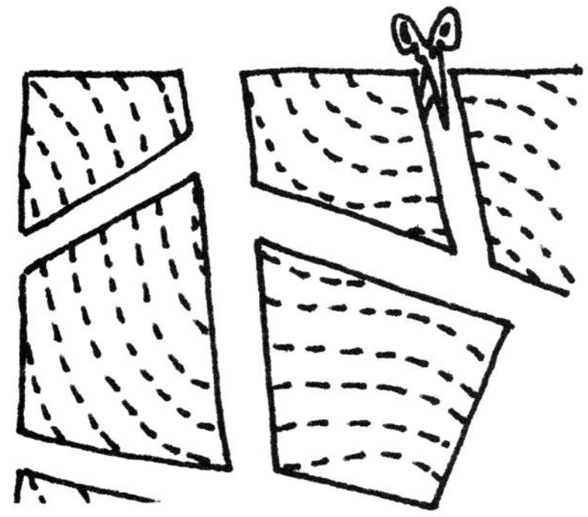

I used very little fabric since the twelve pieces were going to be mixed up in stitching directions and color graduations to make a rather small vest.

This is the Dos de Tejas chameleon vest from program one and this program two deals with embellishing the surface. Mount all these pieces on a backing fabric to join. Cotton flannel or a thinner cotton might make a good base. Cut it in the vest shapes from the pattern and pin the tucked pieces to it, leaving a little space between each. I mixed up the colors but generally arranged the darker shades on one half the vest, the lighter tints on the other.

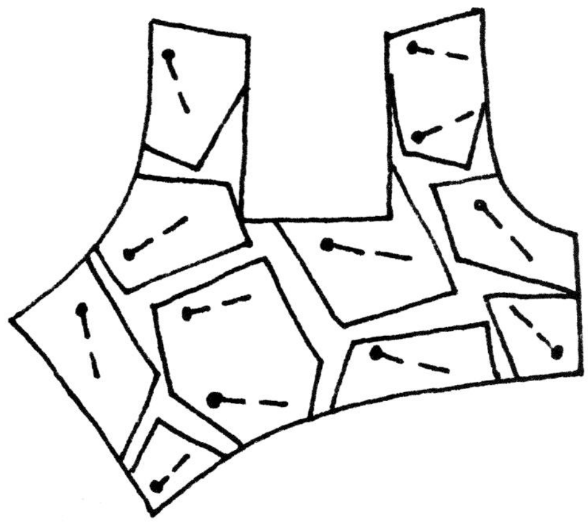

Now comes the really absorbing, fun, fascinating part of the process: Couching a soft fuzzy mohair yarn in variegated colors from purple to blue to blue-green fill in all the open spaces. All this yarn was stitched on in circular motions slightly overlapping all the little fabric edges. The general effect simulates the trees and shrubs bordering and connecting the country fields. With much lifting and lowering of the presser foot and turning of the fabric, you might be able to do this same thing with a braid foot to hold the yarn in place. This could be a very time-consuming process I didn't have to do.

Instead I used a marvelous attachment called a Miracle Stitcher. Your New Home machine dealer this tool. It consists of a foot-ankle replacement that looks a little like an embroidery foot or a darning foot. A little yarn-holding cup clips on the needle screw. Up above a second spool pin is attached to the machine around which to loosely loop a yarn to keep it free of entanglements. Set the machine on a narrow (1.5) zigzag, and thread with clear nylon monofilament thread. Drop the feed dog so you can free-motion stitch. This means you can smoothly do these circular motions without lifting and lowering the foot; without turning your fabric.

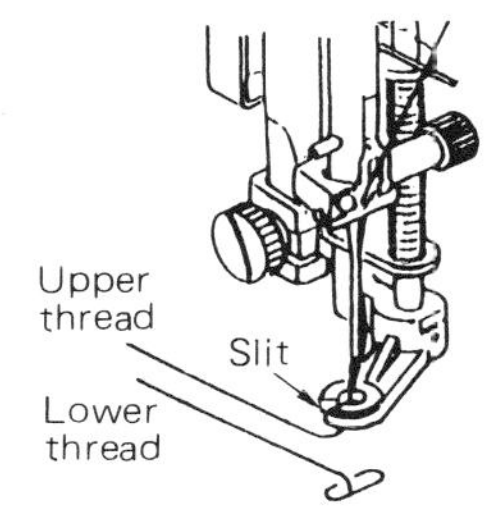

Place the ball of yarn on your lap, loop a strand around the spool pin, and through the needle screw slotted cup, through the slotted Miracle Stitcher foot. This holds it in place while you zigzag over it, covering fabric edges and filling in all spaces with the "shrubbery." Stitch fast but move

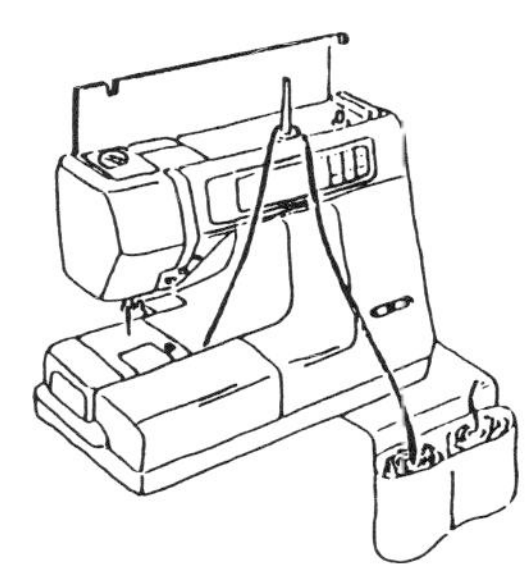

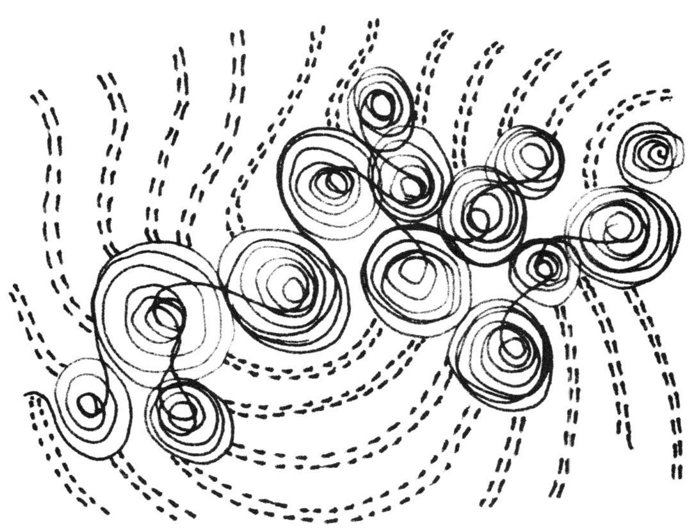

the project around in circles slowly to fill in all the spaces with lots of yarn. Where necessary go back and thicken some parts that want a little heavier foliage.

I liked this Miracle Stitcher so much I used it on two other interchangeable vest pieces but with different effects. With only ***scraps*** of suede available, several pieces had to be used to cover a vest piece. 1" wide strips of a thin fusible interfacing were fused under each joining to the suede backside where it wouldn't show. Then on the right side a boucle yarn was Miracle Stitched to cover up the joinings. The easiest way to do this with a decorative effect was to stitch back and forth in what looked like pine needles on branches.

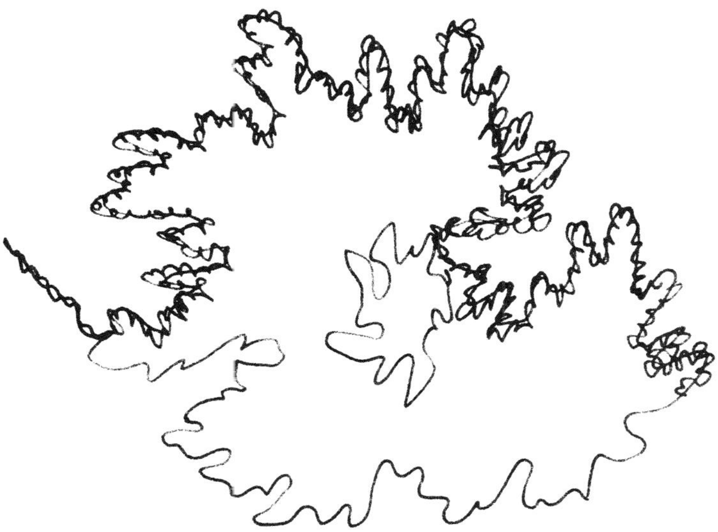

Another fabric was hand-dyed in a splotchy type pattern. Outline these spots attractively in that same boucle yarn using the Miracle Stitcher. If a big slub in the yarn gets hung up in the apparatus, pull it through gently with the machine stopped, then zigzag it down. You can't do anything wrong with this marvelous little gadget and it's great fun to use. Use any cords, yarns, ribbons or heavy novelty threads to decoratively couch on a fabric.

On the flip side of the vest straight stitching branches and little off-shoot twigs can produce a very attractive design. Leaves cut from the same suede and stitched only down a center vein give a splendid three-dimensional touch. Begin by stitching a gently curving line over most of the cut out vest piece length. Pivot at the tip and start back down in a line about $^{1}/_{8}$" away. Start a little twig growing here and there. Stop and place one of the cut-out leaves. Stitch a curvy vein down its center. Repeat this right and left until you have stitched a serene quiet little picture letting it flow and grow as the mood moves you.

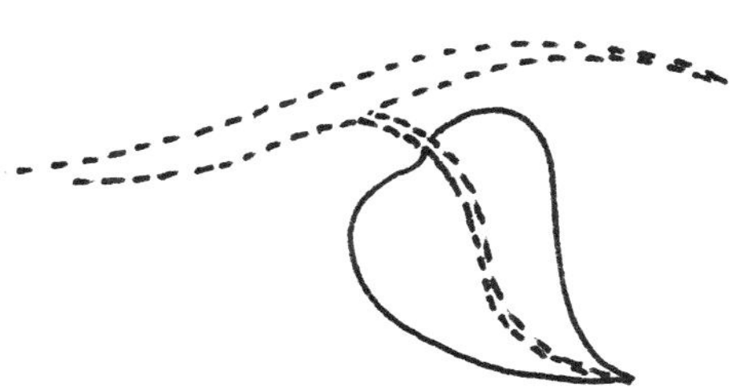

Ups and Downs Program 3

The elevator effect can present big problems as weight fluctuations have you altering patterns up or down. It's also a problem if you are smaller than the smallest pattern that you buy. Some deal with the opposite extreme as patterns do not go up high enough on the size scale. Let's see if we can't find a way to overcome obstacles.

I have a friend who doesn't sew, but when she goes shopping for ready-to-wear, she tries on size 12 only. A dear person she is. A size 12 she is not. She will shop endlessly until she finds something whose styling works for her with a size 12 label in it. Let's be sensible about this. If we can make the pattern fit in a becoming way, that's all that's really important. Size is after all, just a number, and mine's unlisted!

Let's first consider pattern grading – going sizes up or down. Happily most patterns now come in multi-sizes which make them great learning devices. By looking at the spacing between each outline you can see how much a pattern is graded up for each additional size. From viewer letters a common question is, "The largest size patterns is an 18, I'm a size 22. What can I do?" Or the reverse, the smallest pattern is an 8 and you are a 4.

To determine your size, measure your high chest above your bust. Use this measurement to compare with the bust measurement on the pattern size chart. This will be measuring your bone structure and choosing the pattern size closest to this.

Take a look at that multi-sized pattern and, using your ruler, actually measure between the size lines. This amount you adjust per size. Need it one size larger, two sizes larger? Mark the proper amount indicating the larger size on another paper (if pattern will be used again). If this is only for one-time sewing of the project, merely chalk mark this directly on the fabric. Use a straight edge ruler or a curve stick located so curves blend in perfectly for the new size. You can see how easy it is to grade up to a larger size. Repeat this on every pattern piece. Be accurate so that pieces will fit together on your new pattern.

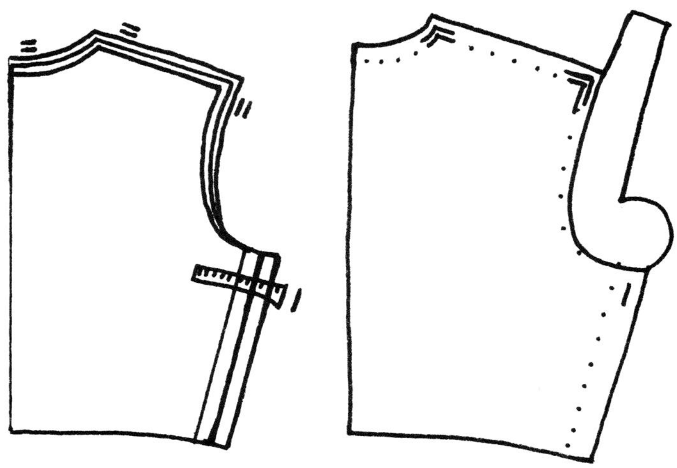

If you need to go smaller than the smallest pattern, the process is the same. Trace this on tissue paper using the ruler for straight edges, curve stick for curved edges and draw an accurate down-scaled pattern.

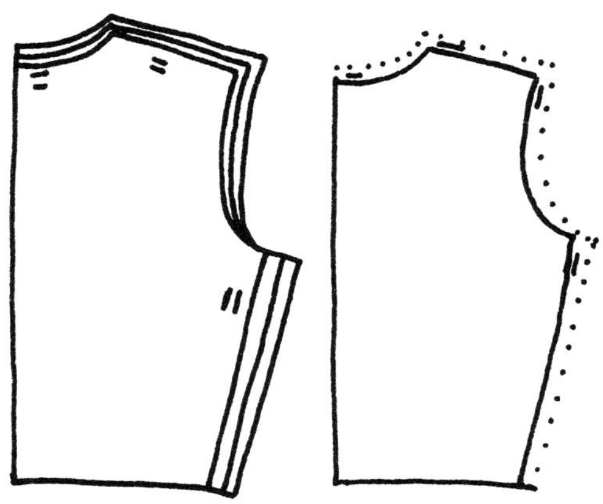

If instead of the paper pattern you use a Bonfit plastic adjustable patterner, it already has included in its size range all sizes from 31 up to 56 bust and hips. You merely look in the little windows as you are sizing the garment up or down. The numbers tell you the size at each checkpoint.

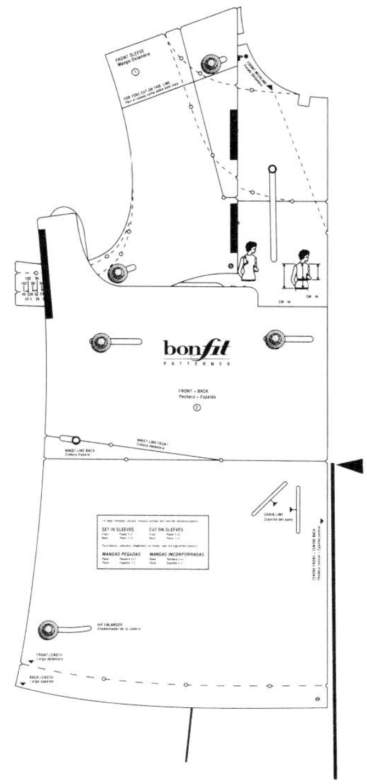

When you arrive at the new size that suits your measurements, tighten the knobs that make it adjustable; it is now locked into the proper size. Merely add seam allowances as you chalk it out on fabric before cutting it out. If you are larger or smaller than the 31 – 56 range, trace the size closest to your size on paper. Make the up or down adjustments the same as already instructed on the paper patterns. Double check your work before cutting fabric to be sure everything will work out correctly.

The Bonfit has a neck template that converts the basic bodice from back to front by simply cutting the lower front neckline without the template. Put the template back on and you have the higher back neck.

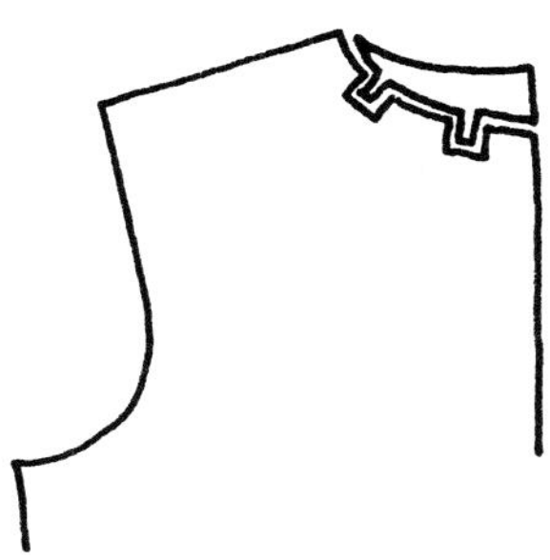

Adjust the Bonfit for length if you are taller or shorter. On a paper pattern there is an adjustment line above the waist. If you are shorter than the pattern piece, fold the paper accordingly to shorten. It would be a more accurate adjustment for your body if you would shorten more than just that one place. If you need to shorten a total of 1", fold up $\frac{1}{2}$" in armscye area, $\frac{1}{2}$" above waist.

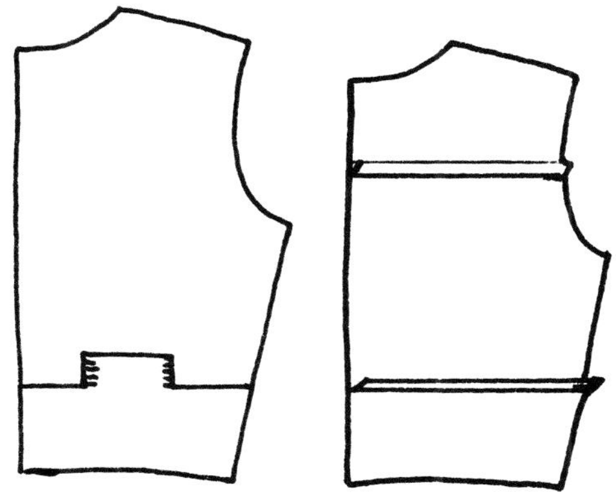

Doing this proportionately will result in a better fit. Remember the same changes will need to be made in any pattern pieces which attach to this. For example, the sleeve cap will need to be shortened the same amount so the sleeve will fit the new shorter armscye.

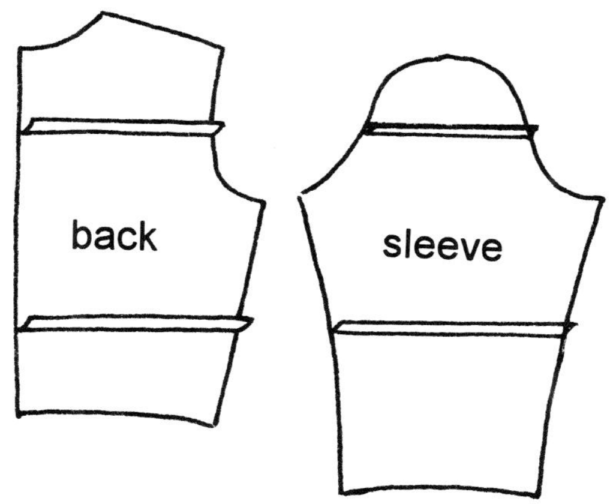

The lower fold may or may not need to be in the sleeve depending on your arm length. It doesn't necessarily follow that every part of your body is proportionately shorter. Compare this sleeve with one that is just the right length and adjust accordingly.

Also stitch that back to the front at the side seam. It may be that the front needs to be shortened same as the back. It is possible however that a prominent bust needs extra length. In that case maybe just making a bust dart deeper will accomplish both. If there is a front facing, adjust it same as front.

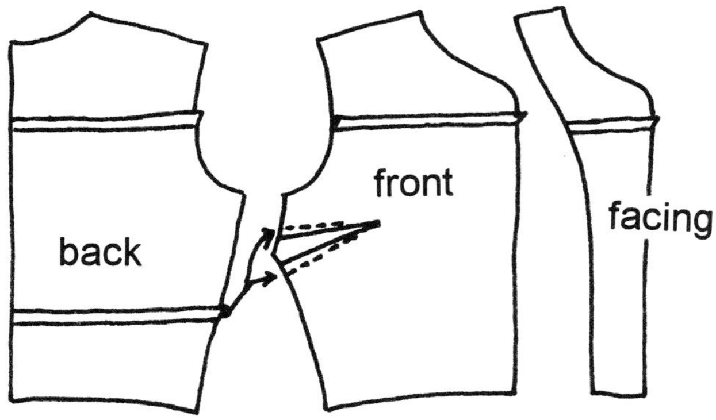

Whether a paper pattern or adjustable Bonfit, some fine tuning may be necessary to accommodate your body's quirks.

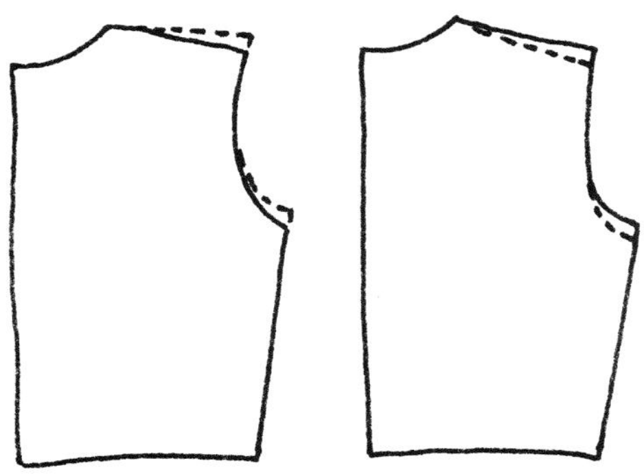

Are your shoulders more square or more sloping than the pattern? Make that change also for a smooth fit. Start tapering from O at the shoulder-neck point to whatever is added or subtracted out at the shoulder – arm point. Add or subtract the identical amount under the arm and the sleeve will still fit.

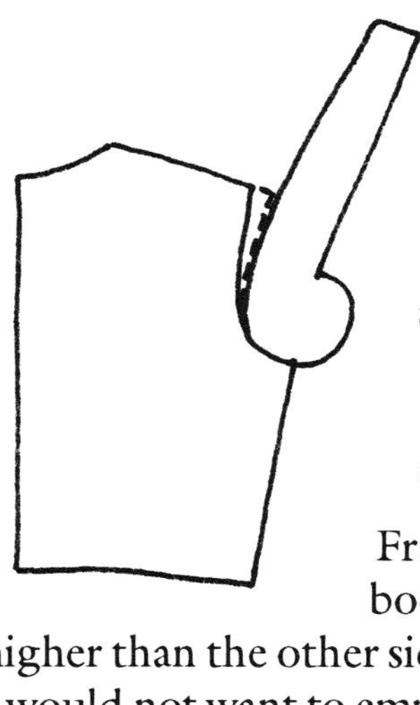

Is your shoulder wider or narrower than the pattern? Use a curve stick to draw a smooth, flowing line. Any of these minor changes can be easily done for a perfect fit.

Frequently one side of a body is larger, fuller or higher than the other side. Wherever possible I would not want to emphasize this by making separate left and right patterns. It is best to make the pattern fit the larger or higher side. Fill that lower shoulder with a larger pad to even shoulder line. A smaller side can have the side seam taken in slightly more.

All this becomes logical as you think through problems and solutions. I am frequently asked which is a better method of altering – pivot or slash. I use both of these plus a few other techniques depending on which seems most likely for the problems involved. Let's illustrate this with a few design changes.

Almost always I start with a basic shirt or pants pattern that is fitted with standard darts.

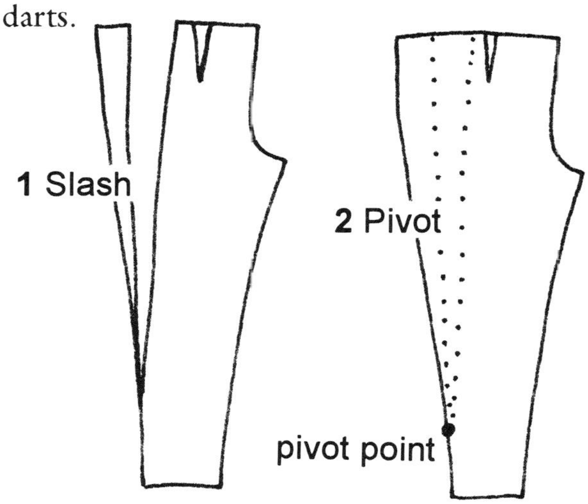

To add waistline pleats, more fabric is needed in the waist and hips, tapering to nothing somewhere below the knee. It would be silly to cut a pattern as in **#1** to add that fabric. The most sensible way is to cut out the center front and in-seam as is, then put a pin in the sides seam below the knee. Pivot the pattern out toward the side the desired amount – 3" or 4", and cut out the remainder. The pattern remains intact, so that's the easiest way. Pleat up the extra fabric.

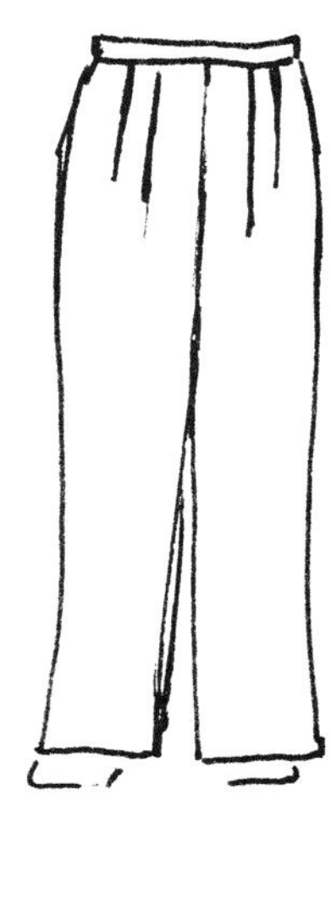

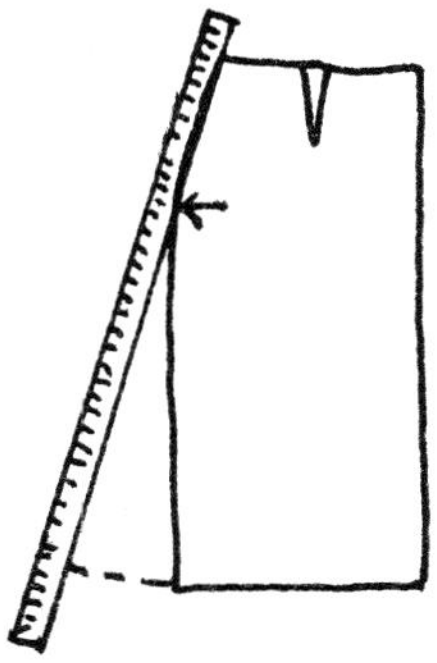

If I want a straight skirt flared, again there is a choice. In this case the biggest choice may not be pivot or slash. It might instead be where to add the flare. Remember that wherever you add fabric down flat on the cutting table, this is where it will appear on your body when you wear the finished garment. We could just add it to this side seam by pivoting the hem out where the hip touches the yardstick, slashing up to this point and flaring the edge or merely drawing the extra on the side with a yardstick and chalk. All of these would be unsatisfactory because the flare would be out at the side only, front and back centers remaining flat and straight.

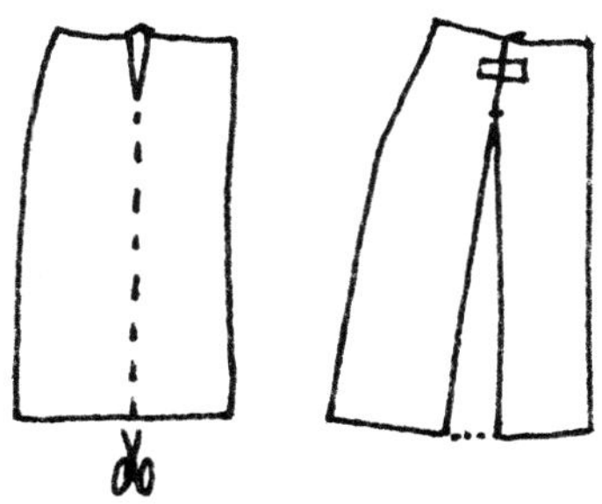

In the interior would be far preferable because, by the time there are two backs and two fronts, the skirt would gracefully flare all over. It is possible to slash the skirt up to the dart point, fold out the dart so that flare opens up – but this needlessly cuts up a pattern. The same thing can be accomplished by using the point of that dart as a pivot point. Chalk or cut the fabric where the solid line shows. Put a pin in the dart point to hold in place. Pivot the skirt clockwise until the dart closes up and you have added flare at the hemline. Finish chalking or cutting out the flared skirt. Notice what happened in both cases. The original waistline was straight without the dart. Eliminate the dart and the waistline curves. This enables a fit around your rounded hip without needing a dart.

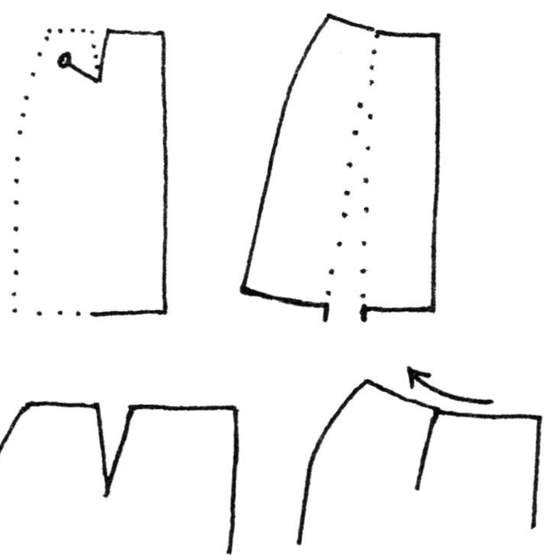

Sometimes you neither pivot nor slash – just move it over. This sleeve needed extra fabric in the center to pleat along its length. Cut out half of it, move the pattern over a few inches and cut out the other side. Pleat up all that excess center fabric until the sleeve is the same size as the original pattern.

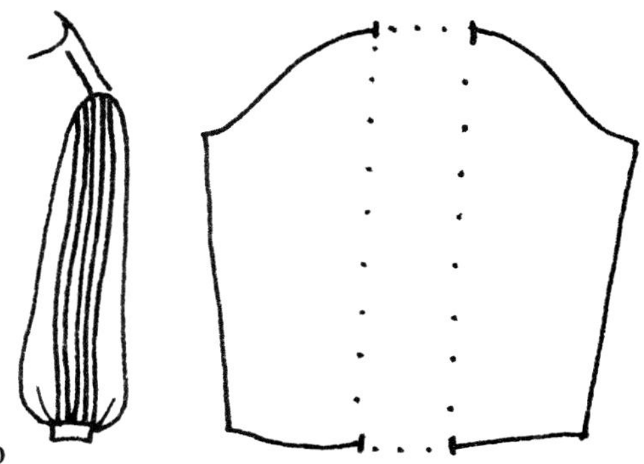

Use this slash procedure for extra fabric at a sleeve cap to pleat or gather. More sensible, however is to use its bottom center – X – as a pivot point, and swing it back and forth.

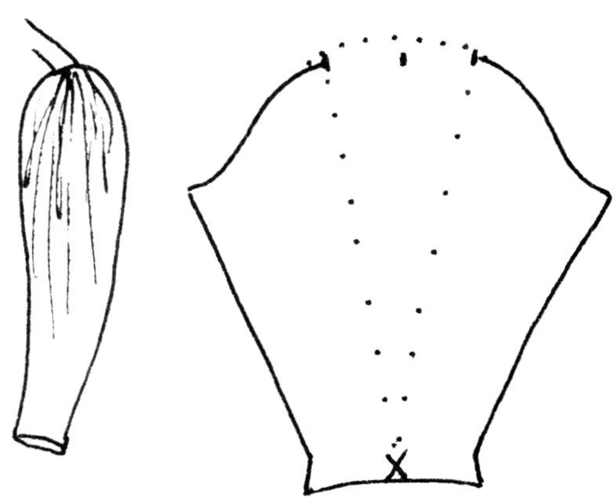

The only time I slash is when there's no alternative. To have a seam like this with gathers below, the only choice is to cut out the top part. The lower part would need to be cut again at its center to spread open a few inches adding fullness. When cutting in fabric remember to add seam allowances where needed. Do this on a duplicate paper, not the original pattern.

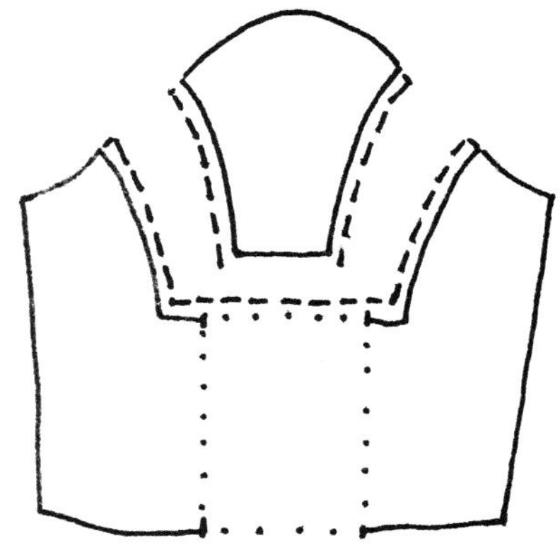

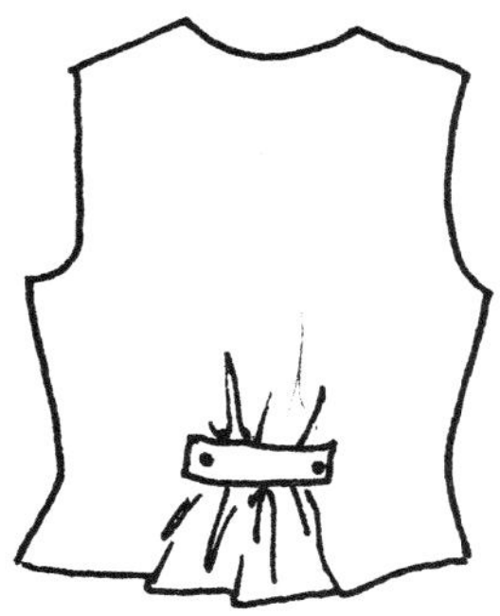

Sometimes your choices involve grainlines. To add flare to a vest back to then gather under a waistline partial belt, that excess could be on the straight or bias.

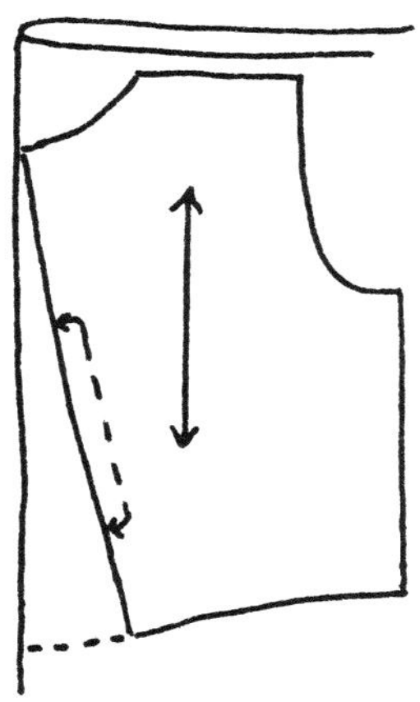

Here it's shown pivoting the lower vest away from the fabric fold. The vest changed grain as you can see.

If you want the original grain to remain, keep the vest straight as you add lower flare. This would also require a center back seam instead of the fold. Either way would work so it's personal preference.

The more work you do with patterns, the more you realize that when you sew you can have whatever you want. Changes are very easy whether it is in the style or in the fit. It is using common sense – along with some of your personal magic thrown in.

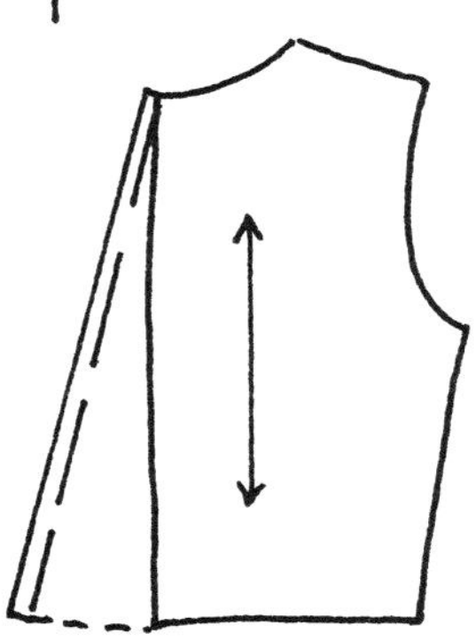

Wardrobe in Miniature Program 4

We're talking small here! Last programs' down scaling for a diminutive size didn't begin to approach this. With an 11$^1/_2$" fashion doll the only thing to do is begin with doll patterns. A fashion doll is about $^1/_4$" the size of a Miss pattern but with out-of-scale proportions.

Donna Salyers brings Fabulous Fur and FabuLeather® within the reach of kids learning to sew. The best way to learn is on a project so simple that success is guaranteed!

Easy projects made from fur are a coat, hat, muff, rug, throw and a pillow. From leather develop a vest and wrap skirt. These are both manmade products – breathable, and washable, but look very much like animal fur and leather. Both have knit backings so will not fray or need any finishing techniques. Cut from the simple patterns and stitch together by machine – or by hand if that is her preference. Rounding out this wardrobe are two rib knit garments – a knit top and a tube dress. These 10 pieces can be made in a day or two. That child will be encouraged to sew more when she sees she really can do it!

All these little garments have $^1/_4$" seams. The rug and throw require only cutting out fur squares – no sewing. The other fur projects will have zigzag seams by swinging the needle off the fabric on the outward stitches. The pieces will open up like a hinge and be flat. The other projects have conventionally straight stitched seams, but can be finger pressed in place.

The rest of the garments and accessories are full size. Mixing fur and leather together makes a wonderful coat. A leather swing coat flared at the bottom was made from a pattern meant for fur. Because of that, $^1/_4$" seams had been allowed. Fur garments are generously cut to allow for bulk so decrease the size for the closer fitting leather by sewing $^5/_8$" seams.

These leathers have a knit tricot backing that provides stretch and recovery capability. This faux leather for pants and slim skirts is a great choice as it easily gives but stays in shape. With about 1" shrinkage per yard, pre-washing is wise if the garment will be fitted. Pre-washing is not as essential for an oversize garment. The choice is yours.

At 52" – 53" wide, many garments can be made without having to buy an extra length of fabric. As happens with this fabric, you may use less than the pattern recommends. Rather than gamble about how much less will be needed, purchase the required amount and make accessories from the extra. Bags, belts, collars, hats as well as fringes, braids, trims perk up fabric these leathers are mixed with. Combine leather with wool, denim, or fur to make that garment special.

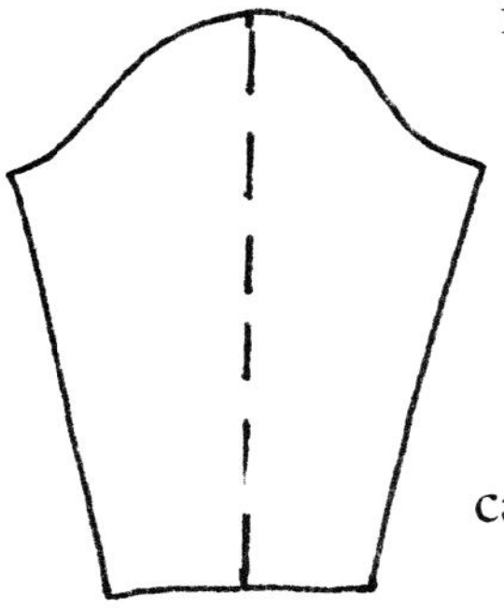

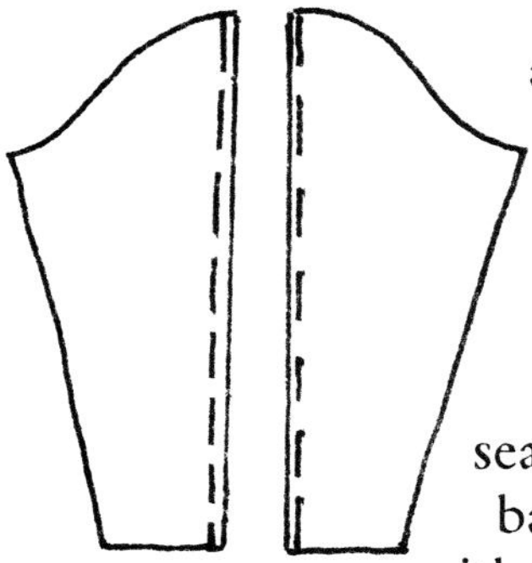

Another way to use less fabric is to add more seams. To cut a big sleeve in one piece might take more width than you can find available. To split that sleeve and put the narrower pieces along the sides of the fabric could solve your problem. Just be sure wherever you split for a seam to add the seam allowances as you cut out the leather. These added seams need not be the same on both sides as asymmetrical balance is quite attractive. One of Donna's coats is cut with the two halves different as illustrated right.

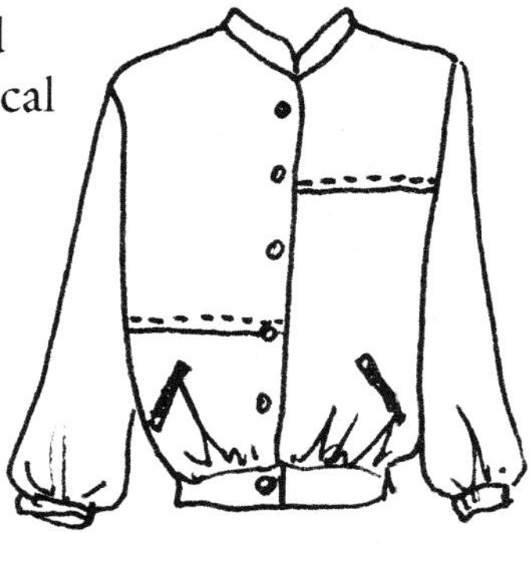

Use snaps instead of buttons and buttonholes for a sporty look. Snap grippers come in a kit, and are applied with an apparatus that punches the holes and clamps the snaps in place. That same apparatus can cut holes for leather strip lacing. A marvelous western collar that looks like a vest uses this technique advantageously. Face the neck line with a second layer of the leather fabric. Draw a chalk line about $^1/_4$" from the edge. Lay a ruler on that, and mark every inch. Avoid having a hole located accidentally in a seam by beginning the marks right next to any seams and working away from that point. (Picture top next page). When all your marks are in place, take a good look to be sure this is

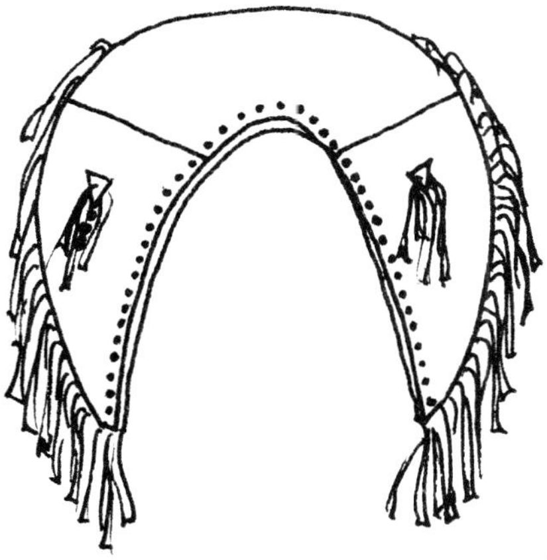

working out to your satisfaction before cutting holes with the snap setter tool.

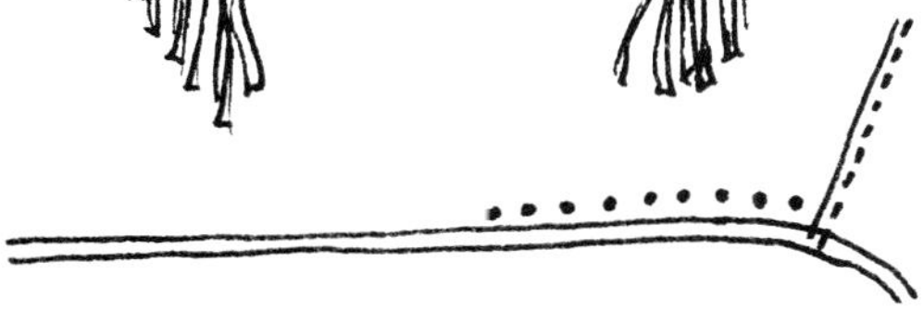

After all the holes are cut, cut a strip of leather about $^{1}/_{4}$" wide in the same or a contrasting color. Trim one end to a point and lace it through each hole without a tool, perhaps aided by long serger tweezers. Another way would be to use a large tapestry needle with its big eye and lace the strip in place. Take care to not twist the strip, keeping it flat with each stitch. This might be a quick fix for a garment that has become too tight with a weight gain. Lace in a narrow panel and it looks as though it belongs!

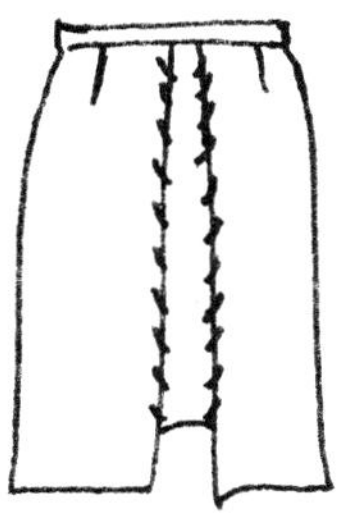

Donna shows some other uses for leather strips. Cut three strips 1" wide, stitch wrong side out, turn over a Fasturn brass tube. Braid these for a beautiful strand of braid that could have many uses. One is to use as a toggle on a fur or leather coat. It could also be a very strong and attractive strap on a shoulder bag. The braid will look fabulous on either side by first making the tubes.

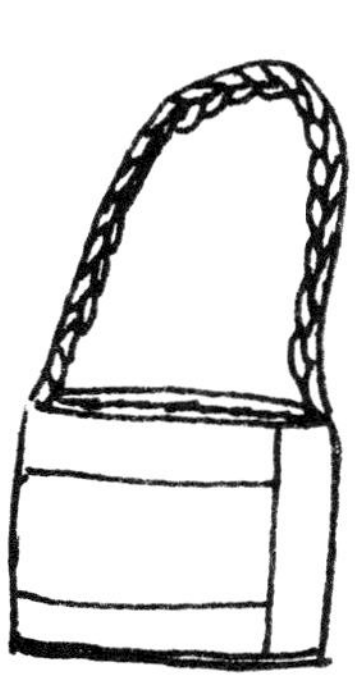

Make this braid flat and it could have still other uses. Instead of stitching it wrong side out, merely fold it in thirds and flatten. When braiding keep it flat; do not turn any of the strips over. Instead cut it narrower, and only fold it in half. I recently saw on a ready-to-wear jacket a braid like this that wasn't folded at all. Thin, flat strips were braided, but not turned over. The finished braid was then stitched on each edge to connect it to the jacket. Practice this designer effect on a scrap to determine the best foot and needle position. It may be an impossible feat finding feet to do the job!

The edge of this western shawl has a long fringed edge. Two ways to do this: **1**– you may cut a fringe on the shawl; **2**– cut and fringe a separate strip to be stitched onto the shawl's edge. Since the fringe is about 4 $^{1}/_{2}$" wide, cut a strip the length needed for the project. To do the job faster, double it in half and cut through two thicknesses at once to save time and effort. Make $^{1}/_{4}$" cuts along its length with a rotary cutter and ruler or shears. Remember the acrylic fringing template used in series 10? This substitutes for a ruler that must be moved at every cut. Position it over the strip of leather and cut many slits through the multi-slots before moving it to the next position. It works with a rotary cutter.

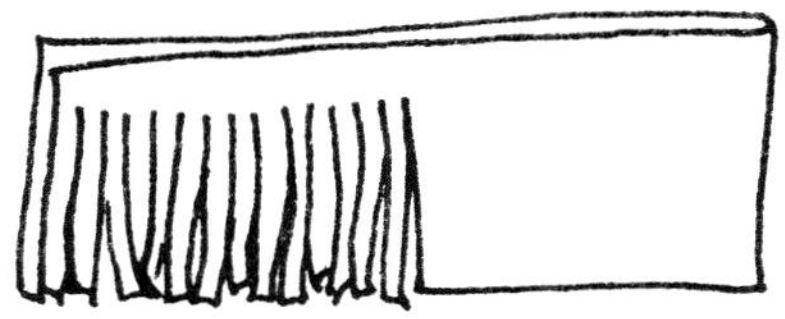

Try (318)984-4869 Beth's Fast Fringer
• 414 Woodvale Avenue
• Lafayette, LA 70503

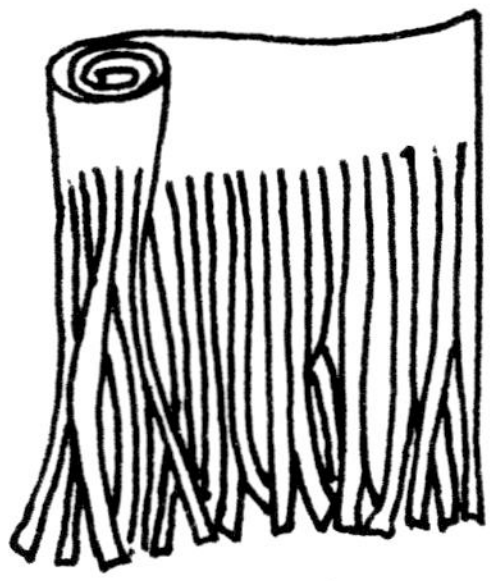

A few inches of this fringe could also be glued along the top edge on the wrong side. Roll it up very tightly and let dry to use as a tassel somewhere.

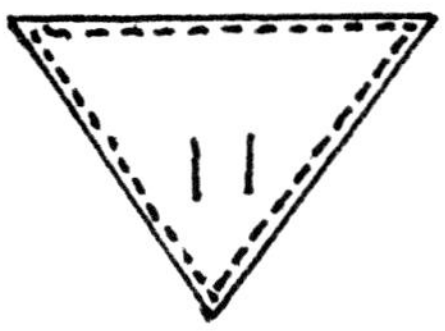

Another little decorative touch on that western shawl is triangles of leather in contrasting colors. They were double slashed in the center, and stitched on the shawl up in the high chest – shoulder area. Pulled through the slashes were several leather strips and a loop of brightly colored beads.

Like to make a grand entrance when you arrive on a party scene? With this wrap skirt in leather, you can't be missed!

Patternless, it is simply the whole 52" – 53" width of FabuLeather® cut with the lower edge rounded at the front side. Cut it whatever length you choose, currently 30" to 36" somewhere down in mid-calf area. It should overlap from one side to the other. If you need to piece it for more width, do that on the underlap side where the seam won't show.

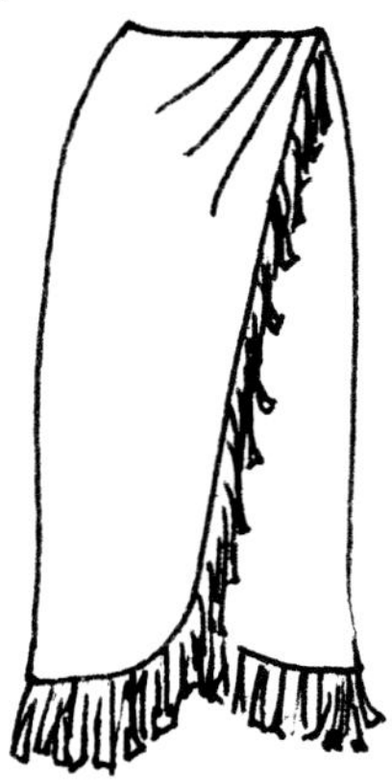

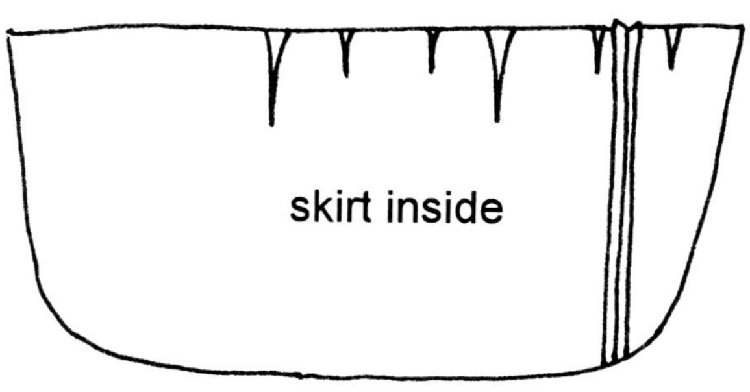

To make this fit well, lay a skirt pattern on it to locate and mark darts, two in back, one on each side, and one or two on the underlap front. ***OR*** wrap it around your body in front of a mirror and pin darts where they work best for you. Take it off, transpose them to the inside and stitch, press. The overlap front needs two pleats for a soft drape in lieu of darts.

A length of waistline French grosgrain will make a good facing. Stitch it to the skirt edge on the right side, press to the backside and stitch in place. Velcro® strips between layers in positions indicated will fasten it. At the open edge, the top layer tucks over the underlap layer and fastens on the inside.

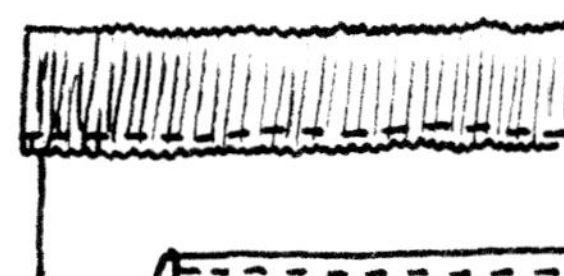

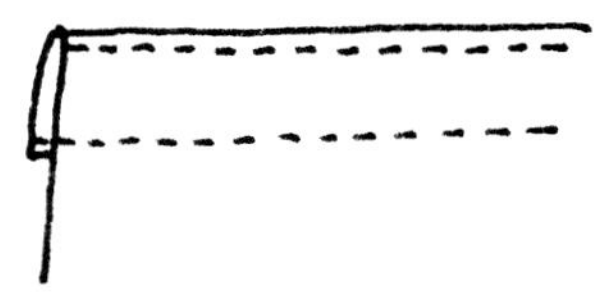

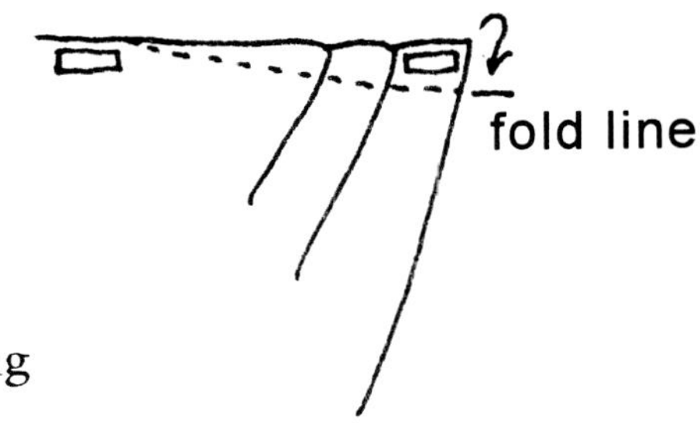

Now for the grand entrance: the more reserved among you will leave it at a big leather fringe all around the hemline. You bolder folks will make a musical statement with every step by sewing a strand of tingle/jingle beads and bells in between the skirt edge and the longer fringe behind. Multi-bright colors with tiny metal bells at the ends of each strand, this is a really festive southwestern celebration just for fun. Patterns, kits, yardage of Fabulous Fur or FabuLeather® and all sorts of notions including the bells are available from Donna Salyers (see inside front cover for order info).

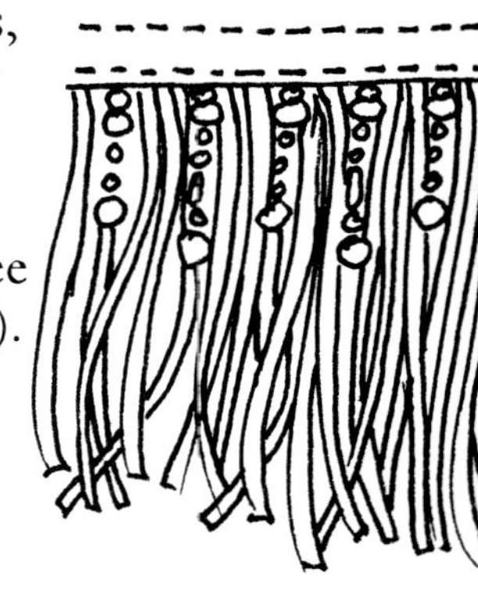

Kid's Art Program 5

I hope you have the opportunity to interact with children be they your own or someone else's because they're such a joy. My favorite little girl sent me a package of her latest artwork. Let's don't stop with merely securing it to the fridge door. How about duplicating it on your sewing machine!

One picture I couldn't resist was painted on a paper plate with sections then cut away so a fish remained – a rainbow fish with multi-color stripes over his body and tail. This was perfect for appliqué, especially when I found a fabric in my stash that looked like a pastel version of a Cubist painting. Move over Bracques and Picasso, make room for Mandy! In that print fabric I could imagine fish eyes and lips and triangular fins and tail.

positive

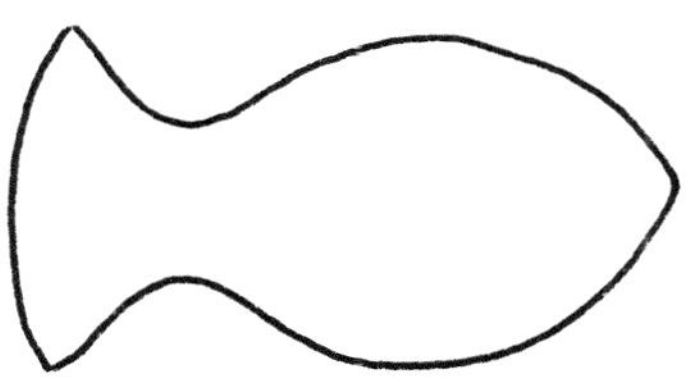

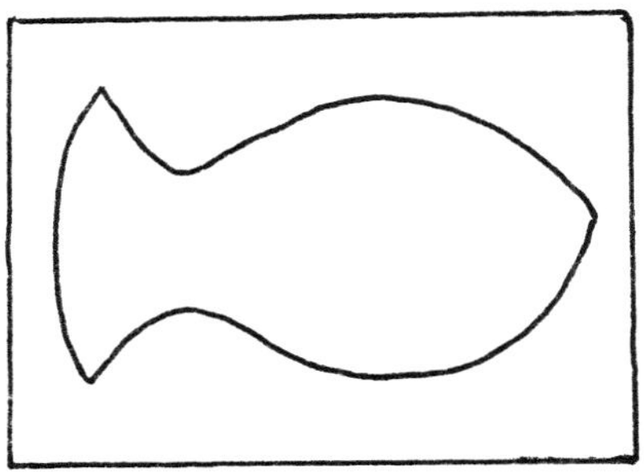

I traced around the fish and cut it out of notebook paper. You'll use the outline of the fish (positive) as a pattern to cut out the fabric, but use the notebook framework (negative) as a window to locate the perfect place on your fabric for the cutout pattern. Moved to the right place, an eye appeared in the right location followed by a fish mouth and a triangle for a fish tail. When the exactly right place is located, pin the positive there. Remove the negative and cut out a layer of fabric backed by a fusible.

Fuse this to a fabric, which in my project is denim, and this fish will be a big appliqué on a jacket back. Satin stitch the edges. Add fins along with eyelashes (little girl fish), and some embroidered shiny bubbles floating upward.

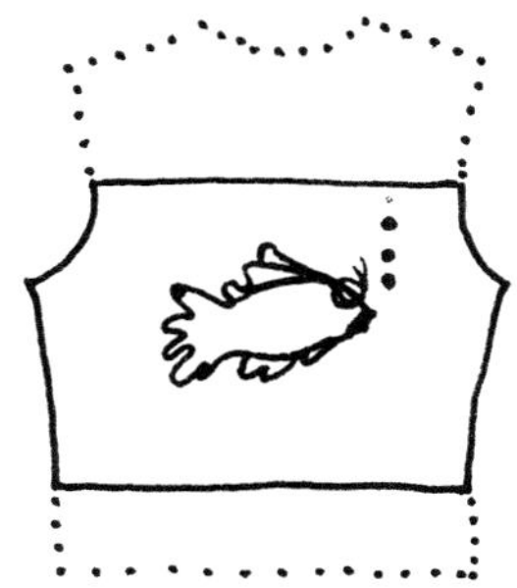

Cut the denim as the lower 3/4 of a jacket back pattern for use as a giant pocket on the jacket.

Cut another layer of lining the same size. With right sides together, sew the top and bottom edges, leaving the ends open. Turn right side out and press. Stitch a buttonhole at the center top edge (illustrated above).

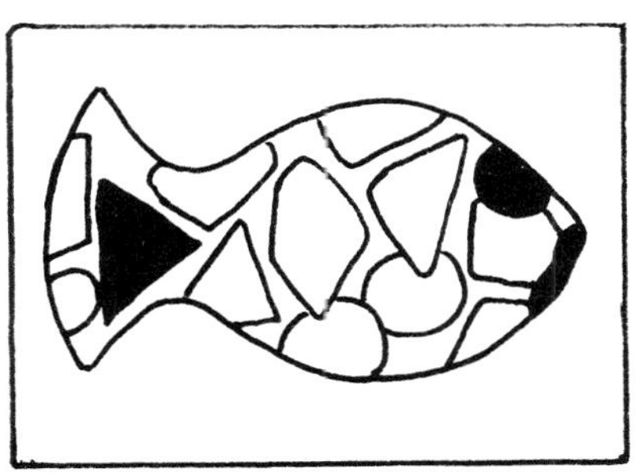

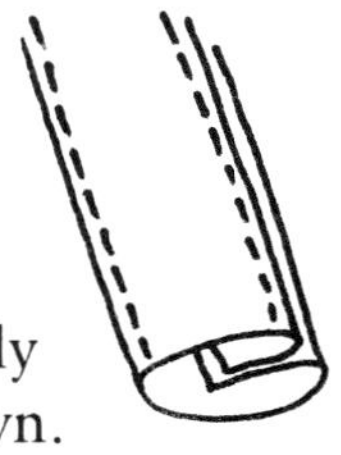

Mount this pocket on jacket back. Cut a strip of fabric 2" x 28" for a shoulder strap. Press it so raw edges are into the center and completely enclosed. Stitch both edges down.

Insert the strap ends between pocket and jacket back up near the pocket top. Stay stitch sides and bottom so pocket and jacket back are one piece. Tuck the strap into the pocket and sew on a button to the jacket under the pocket buttonhole.

Construct the rest of the jacket, put gripper snaps down the front, elasticize the waist and your child has a great little jacket to wear to school.

Why the big pocket? Use it as a backpack when it's being worn – necessities can be put inside. But if the temperature warms up on

the way home from school, unbutton the pocket, and turn the jacket inside it as it all goes inside out. The shoulder strap pops out and you have a great little shoulder bag. Although this jacket was designed for a child, the same idea of a reversible back pocket to shoulder bag would work just fine for an adult in a windbreaker or a baseball jacket of any fabric. If the outside pocket is not to your liking, put it inside the jacket where it won't show when worn. Eliminate the bulky lining and it can even be a smaller pocket on a sleeve or wherever you would like it to be placed.

Another painting from this child was a butterfly flitting about a garden. The whole garden was not duplicated, only the butterfly which happened to be exactly the right size for my scanner, $2\frac{1}{4}$" x $2\frac{1}{4}$". Most of the new top-of-the-line sewing machines work with a scanner, a computerized device which runs over any picture and stores the image on a computer memory card. When that memory card is put in the sewing machine, the machine will embroider the image onto fabric with multiple colors of thread.

Some brands are more complicated than others, but the New Home Scan 'n Sew® is one the easiest – even a complete computer klutz can work it perfectly every time. All self contained in one neat little 8" x 11" package, once you plug it in the display screen tells you exactly what to do.

With a thick black marker, trace the outline of the picture you desire to embroider on the drawing paper (thin tracing paper with a $2\frac{1}{4}$" red square marked on it) included in this kit. To draw a test tracing, use a red marker as the scanner can only read dark colors. When satisfied, trace over that red line with your dark marker.

Since this would be 4 color, after the outline is traced, decide which parts will be the three other colors. With tracing paper over your picture **and** over your outline (stack all three), trace each part individually and color

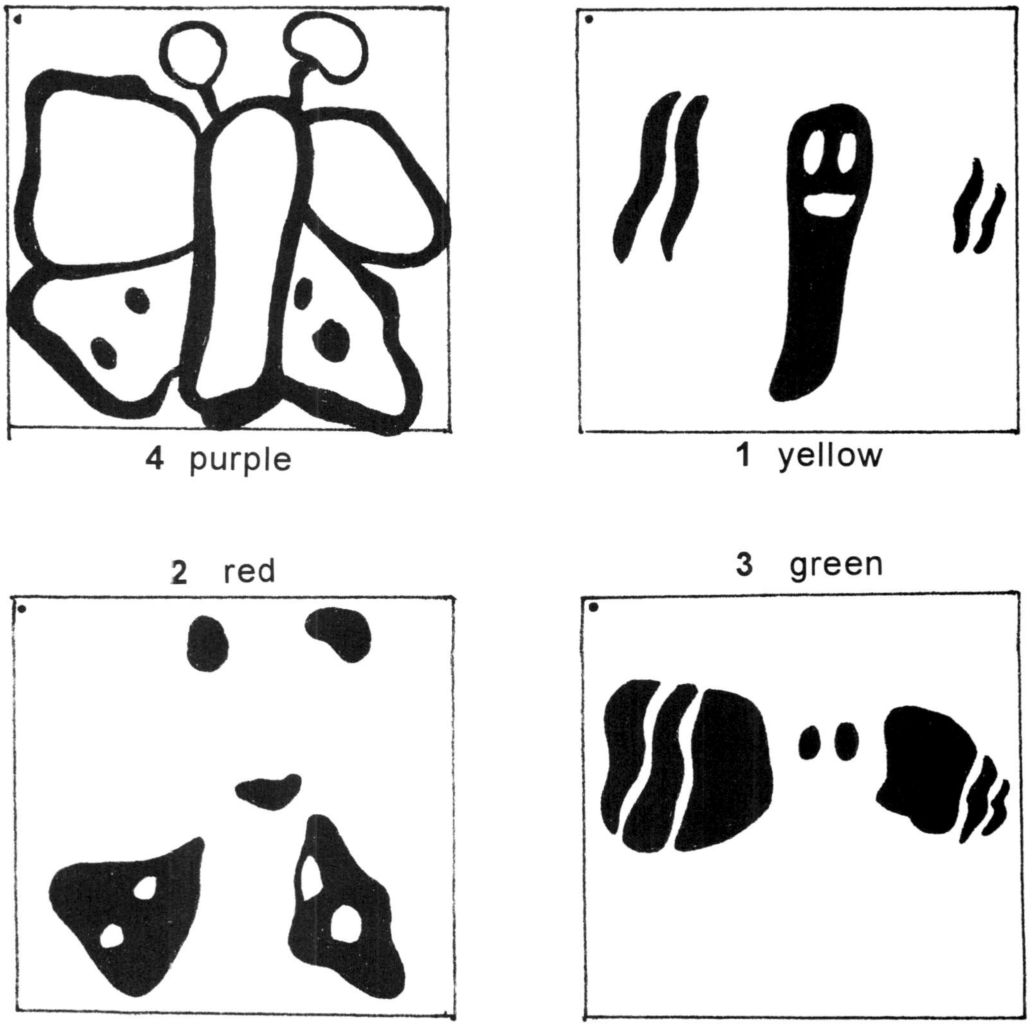

in with your black marker. You now have 4 tracings for this one picture, each one representing a different part and color.

Decide which order and which color for each as you scan individually, pushing the right buttons each time as the display screen directs. The scanner is a little hand manipulated device with a roller on the bottom. It records the image you have drawn on paper as you slowly roll it over the paper.

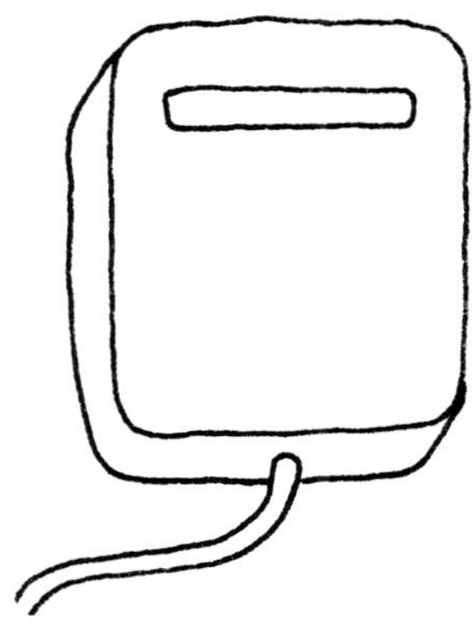

Once you've finished scanning all 4 color panels, turn off the power switch. Remove the Scan 'n Sew Memory card and insert in the sewing machine (New Home Memory Craft 8000) slot. Touch the automatic embroidery button and your 4 picture parts appear on the machine screen in proper order, and thread color labels. Thread the machine with yellow. Disconnect the foot control as this will be automatic. Attach the embroidery frame which has fabric and stabilizer stretched tautly in it. Push the start button and watch it embroider an exact duplicate of this wonderful child's painting! When all yellow parts are embroidered the machine stops. Re-thread with the next color, push the start button and watch the machine do all that delicate embroidery in minutes. The outline was saved for last so all lines will be clearly defined. This is a truly delightful toy!

The kid's art is fun, but think of all the other possibilities. Is there a logo connected with your business or club you'd like embroidered on a blouse or golf shirt? Would you like to have labels in the garments you sew with your actual signature? How about commemorating a special occasion?

My husband was delighted when he did what every golfer dreams of doing – making a hole in one!

Here's what is embroidered on a golf shirt that brings a smile every time he wears it.

Even though this blank memory card is used with the Scan 'n Sew only, a multitude of other memory cards may be purchased. These are all pre-programmed with pictures to embroider gorgeously in the unlimited lush colors in acrylic or rayon thread. They each have the choice of many pictures on any one card. One may be all flowers. Another is every variety of cat imaginable. Another is all transportation. New ones keep coming out all the time so this new capability may be for you.

Working with children's clothes is the perfect place to go wild on embellishing. It satisfies your urge to play around and have fun on the sewing machine while kids love what you produce. All this fun also encourages a new generation of sewers. With their help your imagination never runs dry. Color my world – with machine embroidery.

Drench Coats Program 6

If you have a raincoat you really love, you don't mind nearly as much when those clouds open up. You want it to shed the rain but it's terrific when it works just as well on dry days. Maybe, if well chosen, it can go from casual to dressy and be worn most of the year.

Most fabric shops carry rainwear fabric such as the water repellent nylons. For a child, perhaps use one of these with a cute cotton print for a lining. This could make it a reversible. Rain or shine it would be a serviceable little cover.

Remember the Iron-On Clear Cover® we used on outdoor furniture in series 10? That product can also go into water repellent clothing and would be just great for a raincoat, a slicker. Press this on any fabric to shed the rain, ***but***, once coated, it cannot be pressed. We'll get back to this later.

These choices would be good on casual rainwear but let's think of something a little dressier – or multi-purpose. I really like a coat that can get me through wet weather but I travel a lot. A coat must therefore be suitable for any occasion, any climate, and if possible, any season. Further, it shouldn't wrinkle, would be very lightweight and packable. It should be tough enough to withstand hard wear and when it gets dirty, let's just mop it off with a damp cloth or throw it in the washer and dryer. On top of all that I want it to look rich, elegant, expensive. Sound like wishful thinking? Not at all! Manmade leather fills all those requirements and in a color that goes with everything I own – I'm in business.

Think what features the perfect coat should have. It should be timeless to get year after year of wear from it. A classic trench coat never goes out of style. Wear it over lightweight clothing or big bulky sweaters or suit jackets. Choose raglan sleeves as opposed to standard set-in sleeves and shoulder fluctuations are easily accommodated. Belted, the cold wind won't whistle up and produce a chill. Big roomy pockets are luxurious as well as comfortable. A serviceable collar to pull up for a wind breaker is good. The coat should be long enough to cover a dress even as hems fluctuate from year to year. Print cotton linings for the child's reversible coat are fun. In my coat, though, I want a slippery satiny lining that covers inner construction details and makes it very easy to slip on and off.

Once the pattern and fabrics are chosen, let's consider what type interfacing will work best. This will be soft styling since it's full but belted into waistline gathers so it shouldn't be crisp. EasyKnit®, FusiKnit®, fusible tricot by whatever trade name will be good. It will be on both the upper and under collar, over the shoulder area back, front and

top of raglan sleeves. There must be a large patch to support the welt pockets, and of course a wide strip must cover the length of center fronts. The lower and sleeve hems will need bias strips cut about 1" wider than the hem width. This would add no bulk but it lends just the right amount of firmness to retain the soft, drapey quality.

Then for a few techniques used in it, let's first consider the pocket welts. Skimpy little welts seen on some pockets are not to my liking as very often they don't cover the pocket lining effectively. I'll make that wider if necessary to cover well. Also some pocket patterns are just too small. Wimpy little pockets won't suffice if you can't stretch out your hand and still have extra room. Enlarge if necessary.

Before you sew loosen the presser foot pressure somewhat so the top layer won't creep. Try on a scrap to see if a Teflon® foot will move better. When topstitching, if the faux leather surface won't move easily on the machine bed, place tissue strips under the leather as they can be ripped off after stitching. Use long glass head pins for ease in handling but only the .5mm variety. These fine pins leave no holes after removal as larger pins would. Use a small machine needle for the same reason, a #70 – 75, no bigger.

For the welts, interface up to the fold. Turn right side in and stitch ends. Grade one layer of the seam shorter than the other for ultimate smoothness, same as you should treat any enclosed seam. When turning use a point turner to push the corners out squarely. Moisten finger and thumb and roll

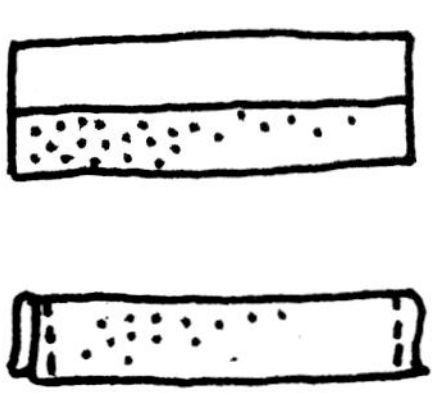

slightly back and forth to get the seam right out to the edge. Set steam iron on synthetic and press with a press cloth. Hold the open end flat with a pin. Remove pin and press harder. Lengthen stitch length somewhat and topstitch edges. The easiest way is to first stitch a foot's width (about 1/4") from the edge. Stitch a second row 1/16" for a second line. Topstitching looks very professional on leathers **and** holds edges very flat – more than pressing alone will do.

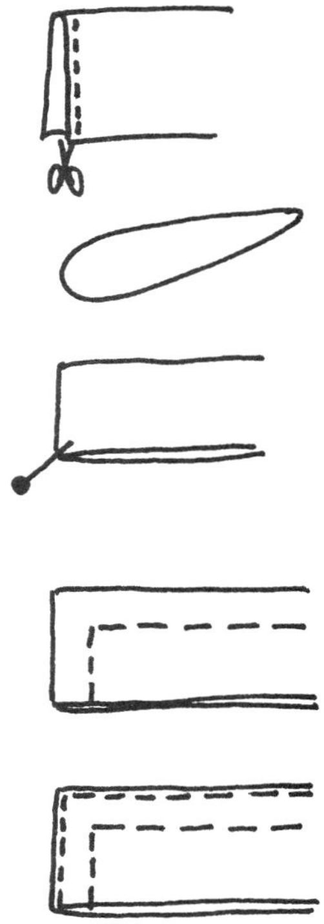

Press open seams over a seam roll to avoid mashing the seam edge impressions to the outside. Improvise a good seam roll from the heavy cardboard tubes that come inside upholstery fabric, if you don't already have one. Saw off to a convenient length (about 16"), and wrap terry cloth around for texture plus a little padding. The rest of that long length save for pressing long seams like pant legs. Pressing a seam, and while the fabric is still hot and steamy, flatten it further by putting weight on a second roll exactly on the stitching line. Briefly hold it in place.

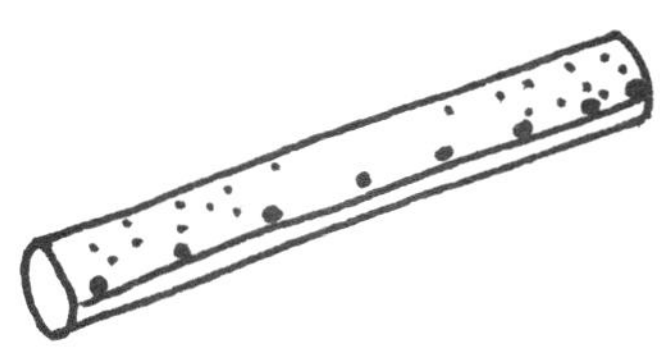

Another tip is to put strips of brown paper (grocery bag pieces) under the seam allowances to shield the edges.

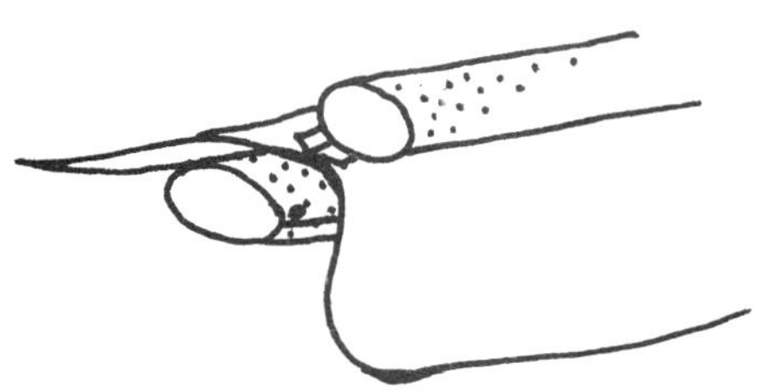

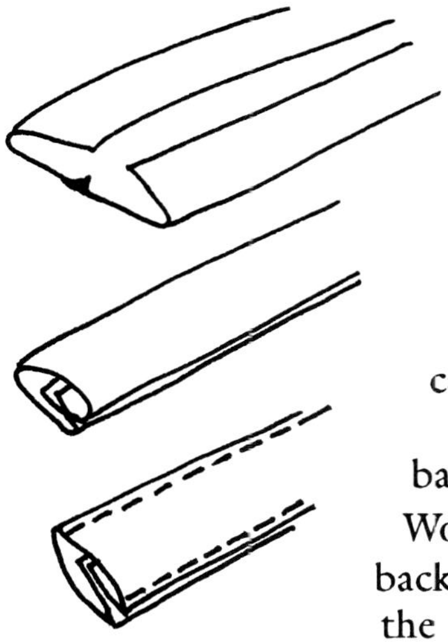

An easy way to make belt carriers is to cut a strip the right length times $1\frac{1}{2}$" or 2", depending on how wide the finished carriers will be. Press a sheet of paper backed fusible such as WonderUnder® to the back side. To determine the exact center, fold in half and make a tiny clip at edge. Peel off the paper and while still warm, fold the two outer edges to the center. Finger press these flat and they will temporarily stick together. Fold again and press with a press cloth. Machine stitch close to each edge. I prefer to do it this way rather than stitching a tube and turning it right side out both because this is easiest and because the fusible gives it firmness.

Stitch these in place on the coat, either inside on the fold under ends, or top stitch from the outside.

A tip for turning the long tie belt: fold and stitch all around ends and one side leaving a center opening. You might want to beef up this strip by first fusing interfacing to one

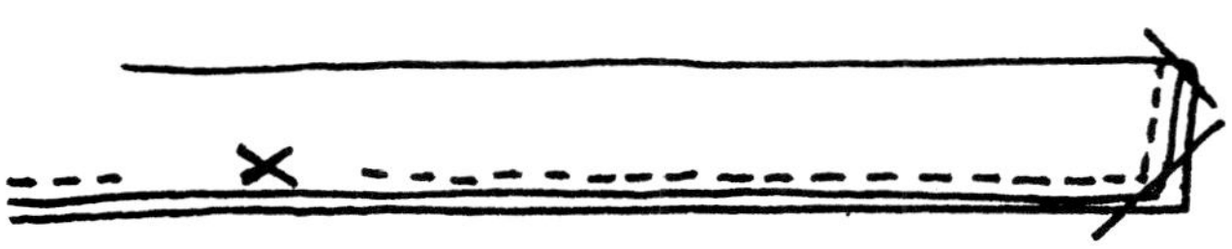

half, up to the fold line. Grade one layer of the seam allowance down narrow, and clip off the corners almost to the stitching line. I only make a $\frac{1}{4}$" seam around this in the first place, so trimming off the second layer is unnecessary.

Turn in an inch or so of the belt on each end and using a point turner, square off the

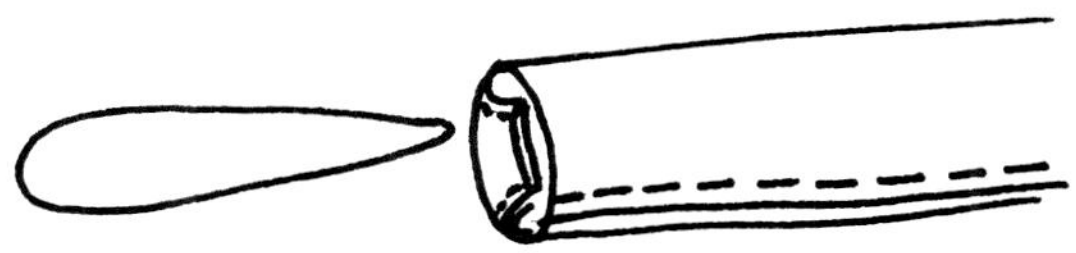

corners so they're completely straight. Then turn the big length over a long wood dowel or a yardstick. Because of the long length this is probably easier than using a tube turner. Before turning, put a dowel inside and press open that seam. After turning, it needs to be pressed flat. This should be an easy job ***if*** you were able to press it open before trimming and turning. If not, it is usually good to hand baste it around the edge before pressing it flat with a press cloth. For hand basting before pressing use a very fine thread – silk or rayon embroidery – so that the thread impression won't be pressed into the fabric surface and show. Topstitch a double row all around.

Flat felled seams either on leather or on Iron-On Clear Cover coated fabrics are a good idea. On the coated seams it would be because you ***cannot*** press once the paper backing is peeled off or it would just stick to the iron. The only way to "press" seams flat is to stitch them flat. With synthetic leather they look very professional with lots of stitching.

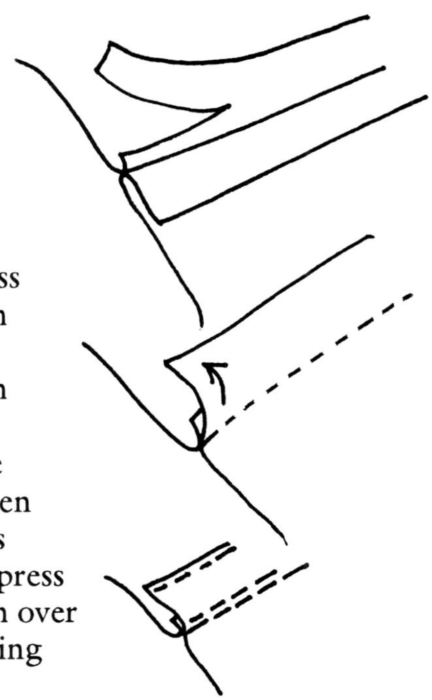

With the leather first press a standard seam open. Trim off one of the seam allowances, the one that will be enclosed between layers when it is finished. Then press the longer seam over sideways, covering the short seam.

From the right side stitch two lines. The first $^{1}/_{4}$" or so (presser foot width) from the seam holds everything firmly in place. The second, very close to the seam holds it very flat. Use treatment with the coated fabric ***except*** finger press instead of using an iron.

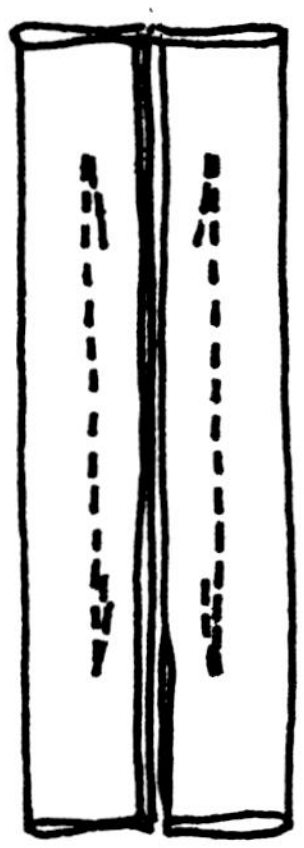

Bound buttonholes are perhaps easier in leather than in any other fabric and look marvelous. Before pressing $^{1}/_{2}$" strips in half, fuse WonderUnder® on back side. Peel paper, finger press to seal. On the right side of coat, position two raw edge sides facing each other. Stitch exactly down center, backstitching on each end.

Slash through the center, coat layer only, and diagonally to ends of stitching lines. Turn right side out, and hand baste two folds together.

On the wrong side, fold coat back and stitch the end triangles down to the two buttonhole lips.

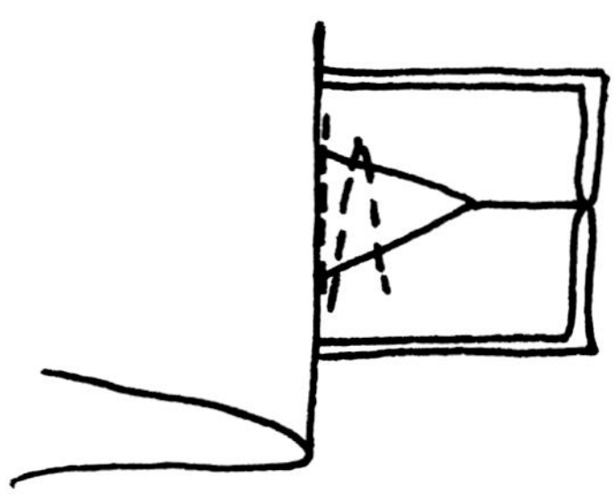

Fit the facing in place, pin all around to hold layers together. Stitch in the ditch all around the buttonhole perimeter. Cut away the facing close to the stitching being careful to not cut any of the buttonhole lips.

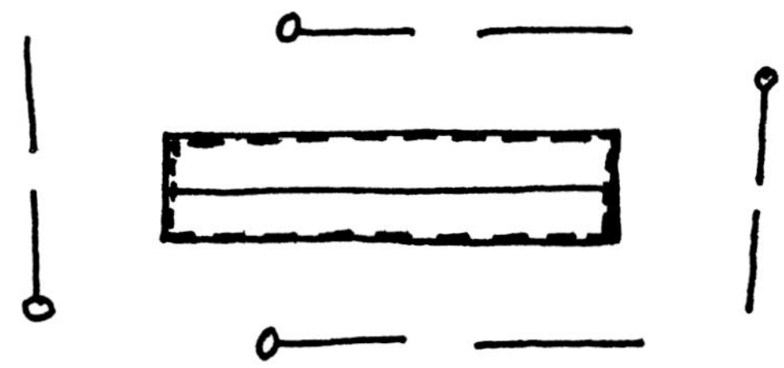

If this is a ravelly woven fabric instead of FabuLeather®, use the same techniques ***except*** make a machine buttonhole on the facing side before ditch stitching. This idea was suggested by Fred Bloebaum of Oakland, California.

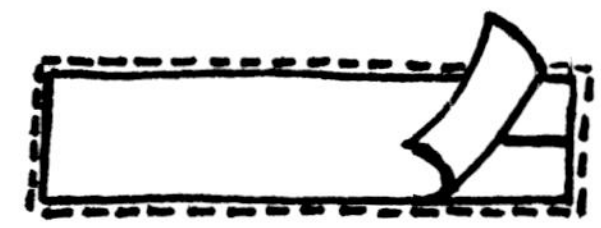

When we taped this program the coat wasn't quite finished because I wanted to show you the dilemma involved in hemming the lining. After that I quickly completed it and now wear it all over the nation. It is simply the greatest coat I've ever owned. The subdued neutral gray has a metallic glint to it, pewter with just a hint of aqua. I love the way a wardrobe blends and intermixes in surprising unplanned ways. From back in series 4 there was a button-off silver fox big shawl collar on a jacket. Much to my delight that collar is also just perfect on this coat turning it into a winter coat. Frankly, nothing is warmer but my neck, but it ***looks*** like a warm winter coat. Since I can always talk John into driving me right up to the door anywhere we go, looking the part is all that's important!

Perhaps every cloud has a silver lining but this silver coat has a festive emerald green lining. It lifts my spirits on a dreary day.

That lining is why I delayed finishing: to show you a potential problem to be aware of. Because the armscyes are low and generously cut, it's an ideal coat to wear over bulky garments. Because of that low cut the lining fabric has much play in it.

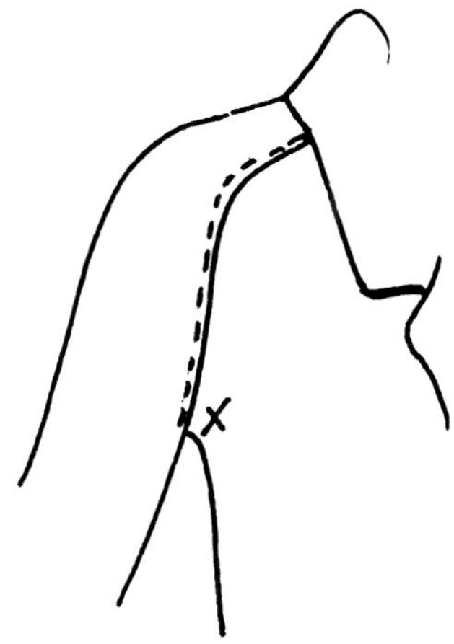

The dilemma was whether to hem the coat and lining together, or to hem them separately. With only pins holding the hems together, I tried on the coat and moved my arms in various positions. I discovered when I raised them the lining was drooping terrifically, which meant it would show at the bottom if left loose. The decision was therefore to hem them together, the finished lining about 1" shorter than the coat including the $\frac{1}{2}$" ease pleat which always must be at a lining's lower edge. A second decision was to invisibly hand stitch all around that big armscye to hold the lining and coat layers together, preventing shifting.

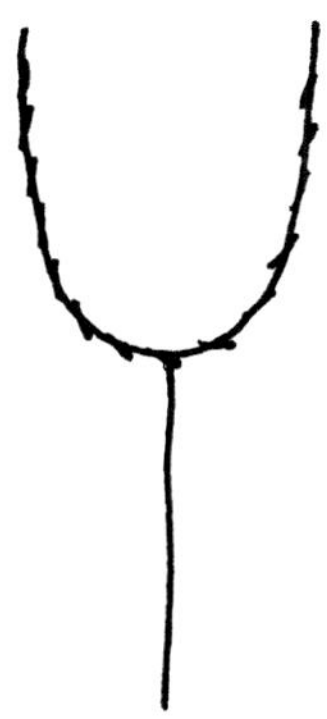

Shear Pleasure Program 7

It can be really annoying cutting out those difficult fabrics that slip and slide and need to be kept under control. For starters, some really sharp shears that feel comfortable in your hand are an absolute necessity. Some of the most expensive shears in my collection are not my favorites. I find myself avoiding them because they hurt my hand! Comfort is crucial and several of the new, mid-price ones on the market are a delight to use – worth looking into!

The most difficult fabrics to cut are the thin, slippery silky types. Chiffon, charmeuse washed silks and rayons are but a few that really test your patience. It is so exasperating when you think you've cut a straight line then right before your eyes the fabric comes alive and moves around to strangely shaped edges! How can this happen and how can you overcome the problem?

Much of this begins in the fabric shop with clerks who cut a little carelessly. I would prefer they tear any fabric that can be torn (some cannot). For the rest I'd like to see them pull a thread and carefully cut along the path it makes assuring that the cut edge is thread perfect. Except for the really good shops with very expensive fabrics, we will see this happen at the same time we see pigs fly! The more typical experience is to see a clerk "kind of" smooth out those slippery fabrics and cut even though you can see diagonal pulls that indicate this is going to be really crooked. If the fabric is a reasonable price I like to get a little extra to allow for the inevitable straightening once I get it home.

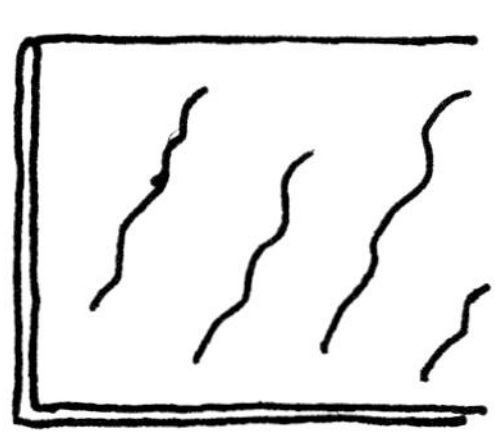

As I was doing a live seminar a shop owner gave me two pieces of fabric that had the above problem. She termed them "impossible fabrics," and asked how they could be handled as she had customer complaints. It was very busy on the spot and I couldn't look at them then. At home the problem was obvious. I held up the fold of fabric to see what would result, freely hanging, at the lower corners. Immediately they sifted like this: 9" – a 1/4 yard difference between the two corners!

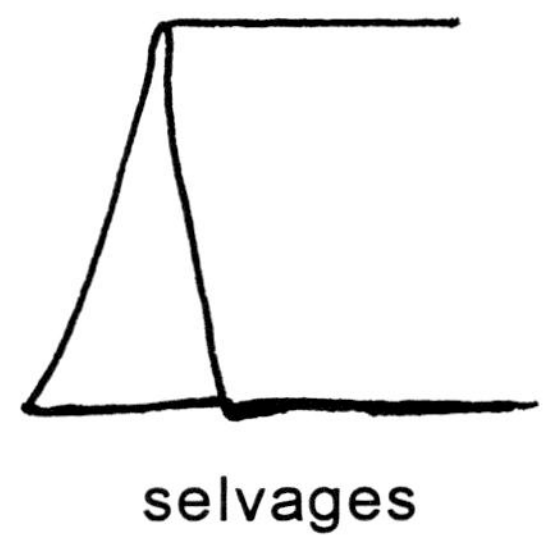

I pulled a thread from the short corner across the fabric, and cut in its path – insuring thread perfection. One thread will ravel off selvage to selvage. When I then held up the fold, much to my delight the corners hung together indicating the fabric was straight, the original cutter was careless.

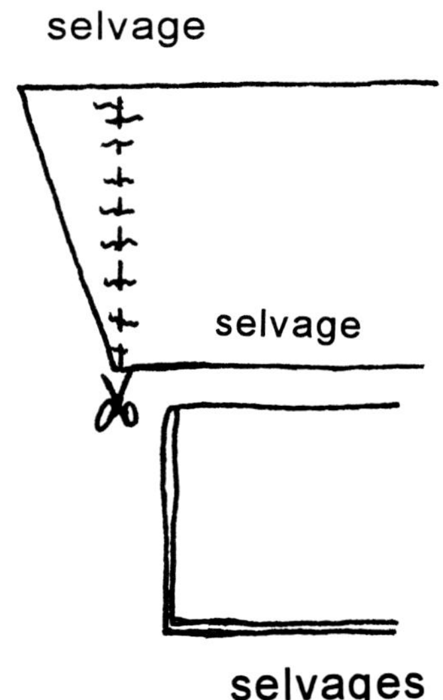

This is the first step. If you do not straighten the fabric it will hang in slight diagonals on your body and will never be satisfactory. Some fabrics however, cannot be straightened. The synthetics (nylon, polyester,

1101 - Four parts to each chameleon vest, they can mix and match many ways for wardrobe versatility

1104 - Donna Salyer's Fabulous Fur and FabuLeather make a 10 piece fabulous wardrobe for a fashion doll.

1101 - A closer look at Karen Odam's Dos de Tejas vests and skirts. Wonderful fabric mixes can go in these skirts!.

1102 - Dos de Tejas pattern, the fabric combinations, usage, embellishments were the challenge. Any kind of fabric will work.

1104 - Big long fringes are great on faux leather wrap skirts and big collars. Mix in some fur and beads for the fun of it.

1106 - My favorite trench coat for rain or shine, everyday or dress up. Faux leather can't be beat for good looks and practicality.

1107 - Byrnece Mefford of Kearney, NE, made this blooming jacket. Multi-layers of fabric are slashed between stitching lines.

1109 - A simply cut jacket with unbroken lines is beautiful on petite Byrnece Mefford. A larger person would look narrower with the addition of shoulder flanges.

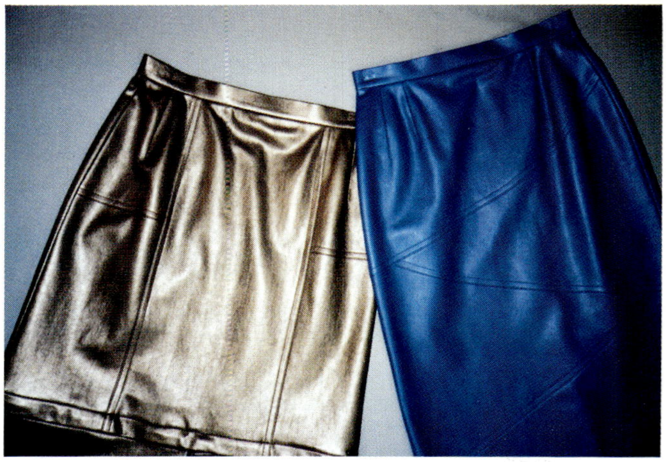

1109 - Made from a basic skirt pattern, adding extra seams breaks up large spaces to diminish body size.

1108 - A reversible vest from Kathy Smith of Rochester, NY, is generously stitched on cotton coordinates.

1108 - Crinkling, fusing, metallic stitching make this fish print cotton look like silk.

1108 - Contemporary log cabin quilting adds an appropriate print here and there to coordinate the vest with several other garments.

1111 - This Tibetan jacket begins as a simple rectangle for the body area. Enormous sleeves whose armscyes extend all the way down to the hips are added.

1110 - The challenge in all these garments is placement of design when laying the pattern.

1110 - Sheets by Ralph Lauren joined a Folkwear pattern to make this fabulous coat by Vona Marengo of Worster, MA.

1112 - Beautiful silk inside and out, this version of the Tibetan jacket belongs to Louise Mensing of Virginia. Note the zip-out sleeves which convert it to a vest.

1110 - Fred Bloebaum's coat began as a Ralph Lauren blanket. A cotton Indian sari provided all the fabric in this Suzanne Klemenz suit.

1113 - Louise's jacket again, one sleeve zipped out. The black melton also zips apart and combines with a leather as well as a fur jacket.

Behind the scenes – truly amazing how quickly the models change into each different outfit as the video cameras keep them all busy.

acrylic, etc.) are heat set in this shape and cannot usually be changed. On the natural fibers (cotton, linen, silk, wool), you can usually pull the short corners once it is cut thread perfect, and make it grain perfect.

After straightening, pre-shrinking if necessary, the cutting of these slipperies can still be difficult. A sure way to prevent distortion is to first lay down newspapers, single thickness. Position the fabric on them, lining up square edges. Lay the pattern and pin through all layers. Cut through everything including the newspaper. You'll be delighted at how nothing moves. Your cutting will be very accurate!

When cutting light to medium weight fabrics, which is probably most of the time, there are several shears on the market with just slightly (microscopically) serrated blades so the fabric won't slip away. For those of you with slightly arthritic hands, try out the Fiscar spring operated soft cutter shears. Completely unlike shears we've always used, these have a spring action making it very easy to manipulate. Your hand pushes down but the spring automatically opens them back up making them gentle on the hand. A small version is identical and takes care of the little snips.

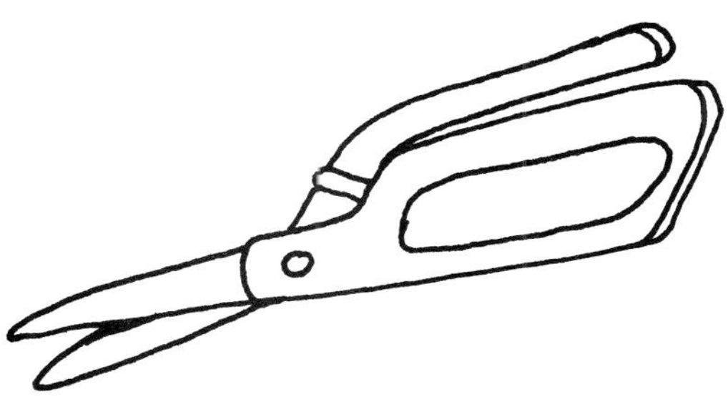

Others are strictly heavy duty for the thick, tough fabrics. These you really want to try before you buy. Well designed handles make a world of difference between comfort and blisters. Bent shears are usually easier to operate than straight designs because the lower blade is flat on the table.

Cutting faux fur doesn't require these heavy cutters because you don't cut through it all. Simply cut through the knit backing, omitting the fur. This means what is most important are sharp points. Cut ***against*** the pile because the sharp under point parts the hair and cleanly cuts knit only.

Some interesting rotary cutters have changed a little in case you haven't seen them lately. Pro Cut® has a rechargeable electric one that operates without a cutting mat. It can cut through anything without any effort and cuts against its small attached platform.

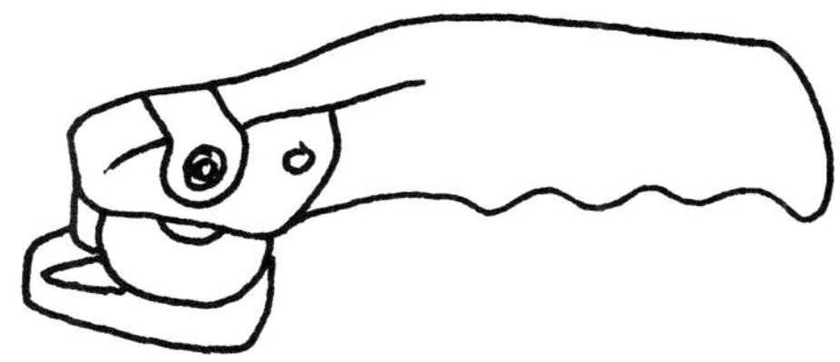

Fiscars® has a paper cutter that also cuts fabric. As a whole it looks like a paper cutter you've always seen. However this has a rotary blade that pushes back and forth instead of the usual arm blade that raises and lowers.

Look also for a comfortable rotary cutter that fits the hand and provides leverage. Two extra interchangeable blades offer the other alternatives of a wave cut and pinking cut.

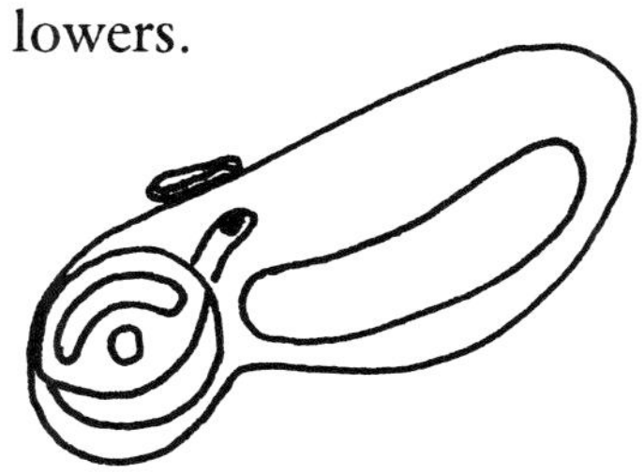

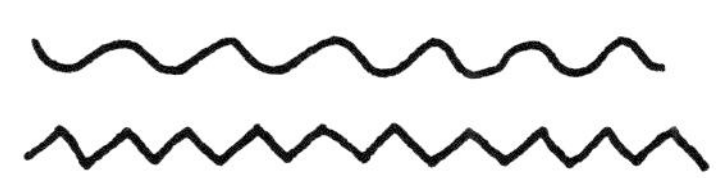

With cutting in mind let us revive an old idea that may interest you for some fun cutting.

A "blooming" garment is one that has several layers of fabric all stitched together, usually in parallel row. Most layers are then slashed open between the stitching lines, leaving only the bottom layer intact. I made a sweatshirt for my favorite granddaughter in this manner in series 7.

Think of the fabrics you might use in this. An easy way to arrive at a color scheme is to choose a print for one layer, then use its colors to coordinate all the other layers. Slash all these fabrics and only the fabric edges show. This gives a hint of fabrics used but if the color is right, think of burying in the melange a layer or two from your collection – you may even be able to find a use for that awful piece you bought years ago!

A pretty jacket photographed is on loan from Byrnece Mefferd, the American Sewing Guild administrator from Kearney, Nebraska. The surface is blue but a print is down deep in it. A matching rayon challis skirt and blouse ties the whole outfit together beautifully.

If using prints, avoid those printed very dark on the right side, light on the back side. It is better to choose something with a similar light-dark value on both sides since the edges flip over and you really don't want the big contrast to show.

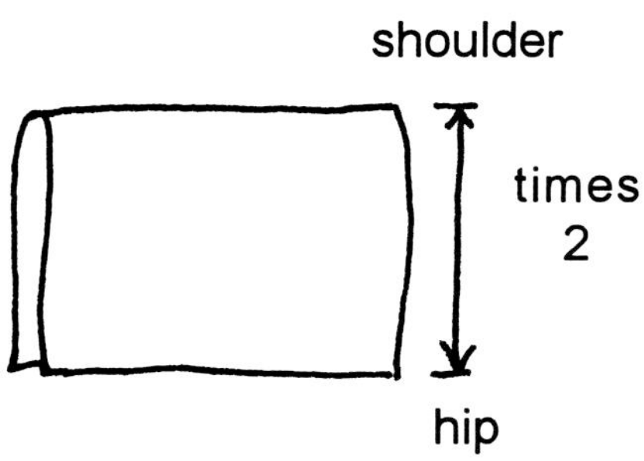

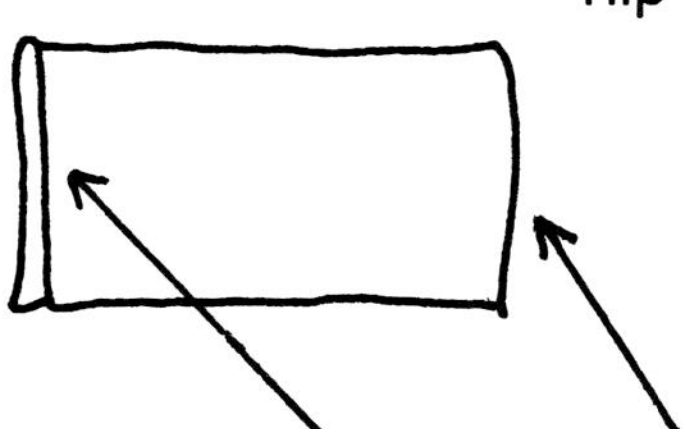

Basically this is how the jacket is made. Fold the fabric in half, the length twice the amount it takes to go from shoulder to hip. The width is from selvage to selvage. As that would fit on your body, it would mean about elbow length for 45" fabric. To be wrist length, you would need 54" or 60" fabric in the other direction. For 45" fabric it would end a few inches below your waist if that's long enough. Then for the below-elbow length, buy $1\frac{1}{4}$ yard of each fabric layer to be used. For wrist length buy $1\frac{1}{2}$–$1\frac{5}{8}$ yard.

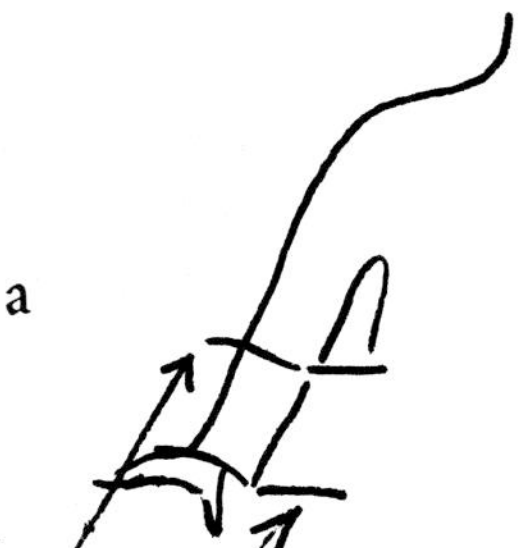

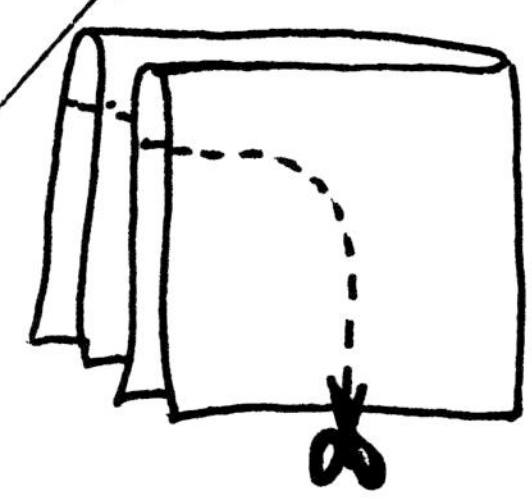

Eventually the fabric will be folded the other direction with the underarm area being cut out. I've previously made other patternless jackets or blouses. Other measurements needed are sleeve width (how wide do you want them to be? At least big enough for hand to go through at wrist).

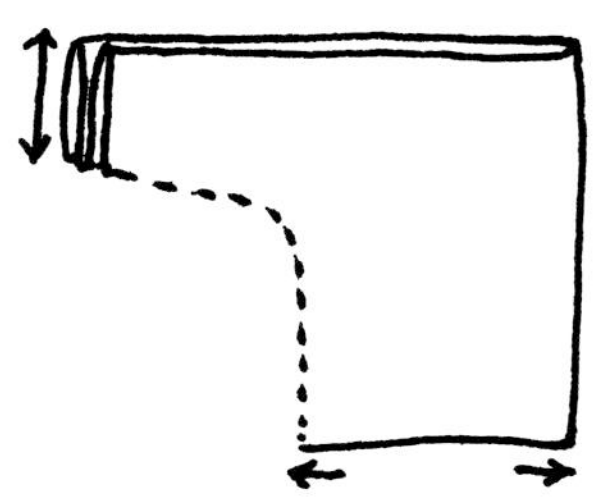

1/4 hips

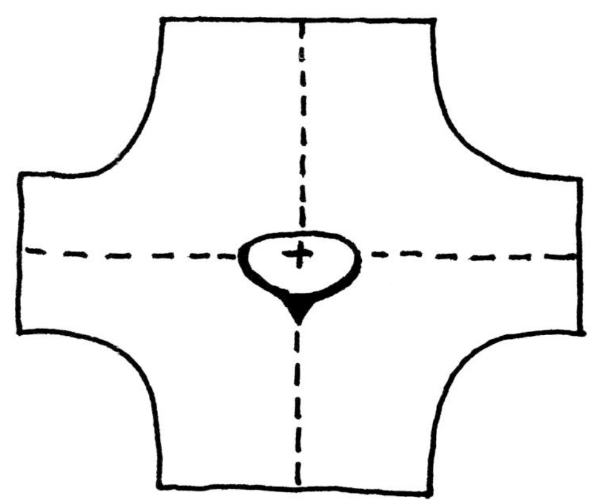

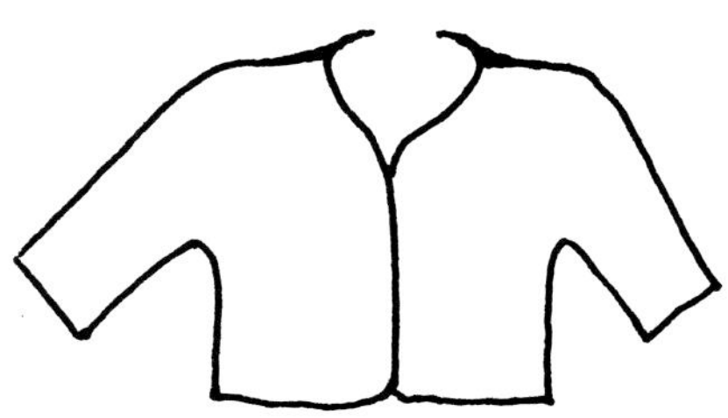

The lower measurement is 1/4 the width of your hip area at that level (plus ease) since you have four layers. When all stitched and ready to finish up, slash the front open and cut out neckline oval. Finishing into a jacket will end the project.

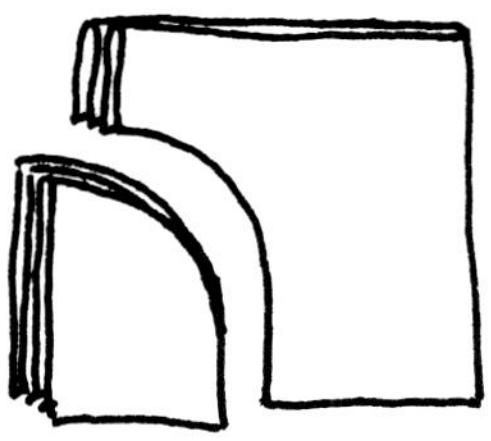

To begin the work once you've designed a plan, fold the top layer of fabric in whatever dimensions you chose. Cut out the underarm area.

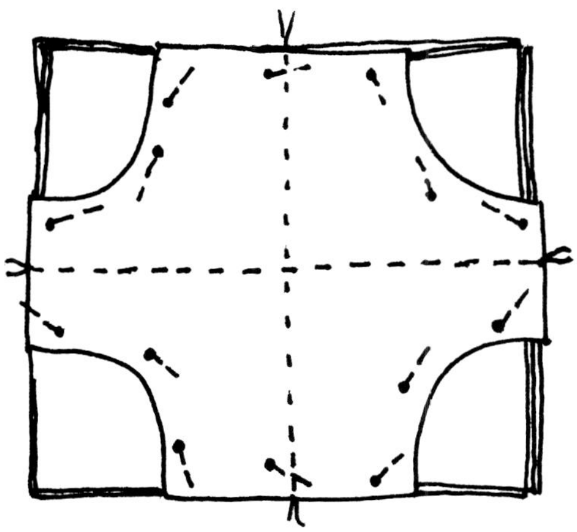

Now position that on top of the other stacked layers and a few pins will hold it in place. Using this as a pattern, cut out the rest of the underarm areas. ¤Note: it would frankly be easier to ***not*** cut these out at this time. To wait until all stitching is complete before doing any cutting is easier, but in the interest of saving all that corner fabric for other projects, cutting now is the frugal way.¤

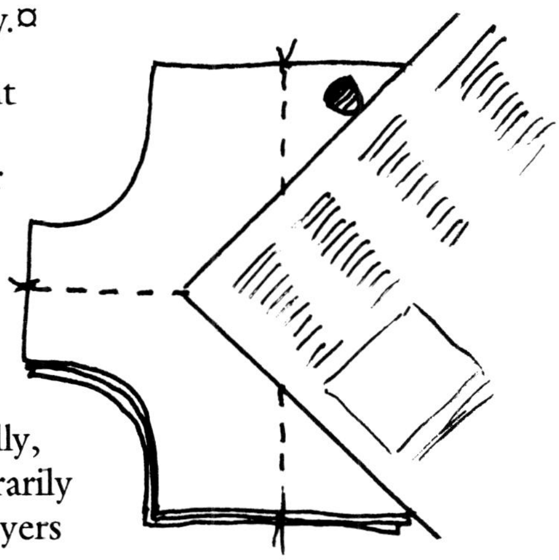

Baste right through the center of the stacked pieces, vertically and horizontally, to temporarily hold all layers together as one.

Lay a newspaper on the project diagonally so that its point is right on one of the basted lines, its edges running through two fabric corners. This is using the paper as an **L** square. Mark this line with a chalk wheel.

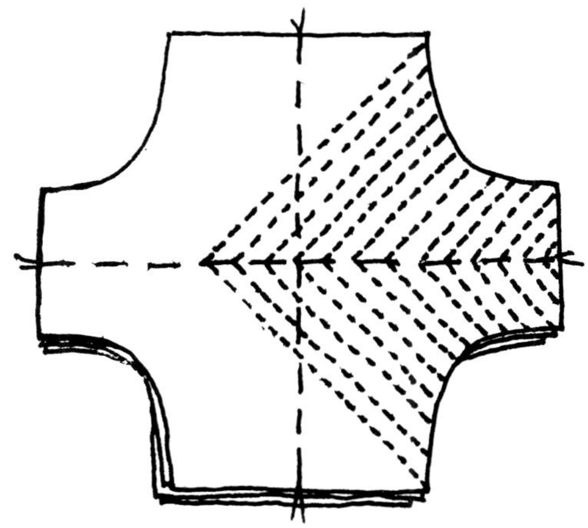

Stitch this line with normal size stitches. They will be permanent. Now stitch off the rest in parallel lines either by marking them all, or by using a quilting gauge in the machine to make evenly spaced lines. Byrnece stitched hers 1" apart. Remove any pins before you come to them. If any of the fabric layers seem to be shifting, loosen presser foot pressure. If stitching through all these layers seems tough, use a jeans needle to more easily penetrate.

For the rest of the jacket, mark and stitch the other direction. Using this template or a neckline design of your own, position it as instructed on project.

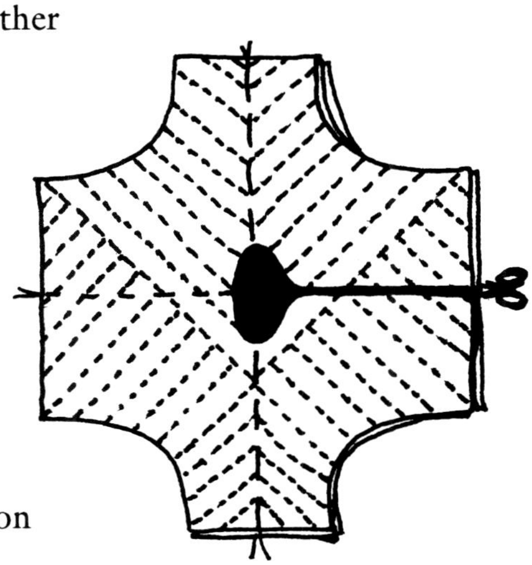

Cut up the center front (on basting line) and around the neck. Discard neck piece, and remove basting lines from shoulder horizontal and center back vertical.

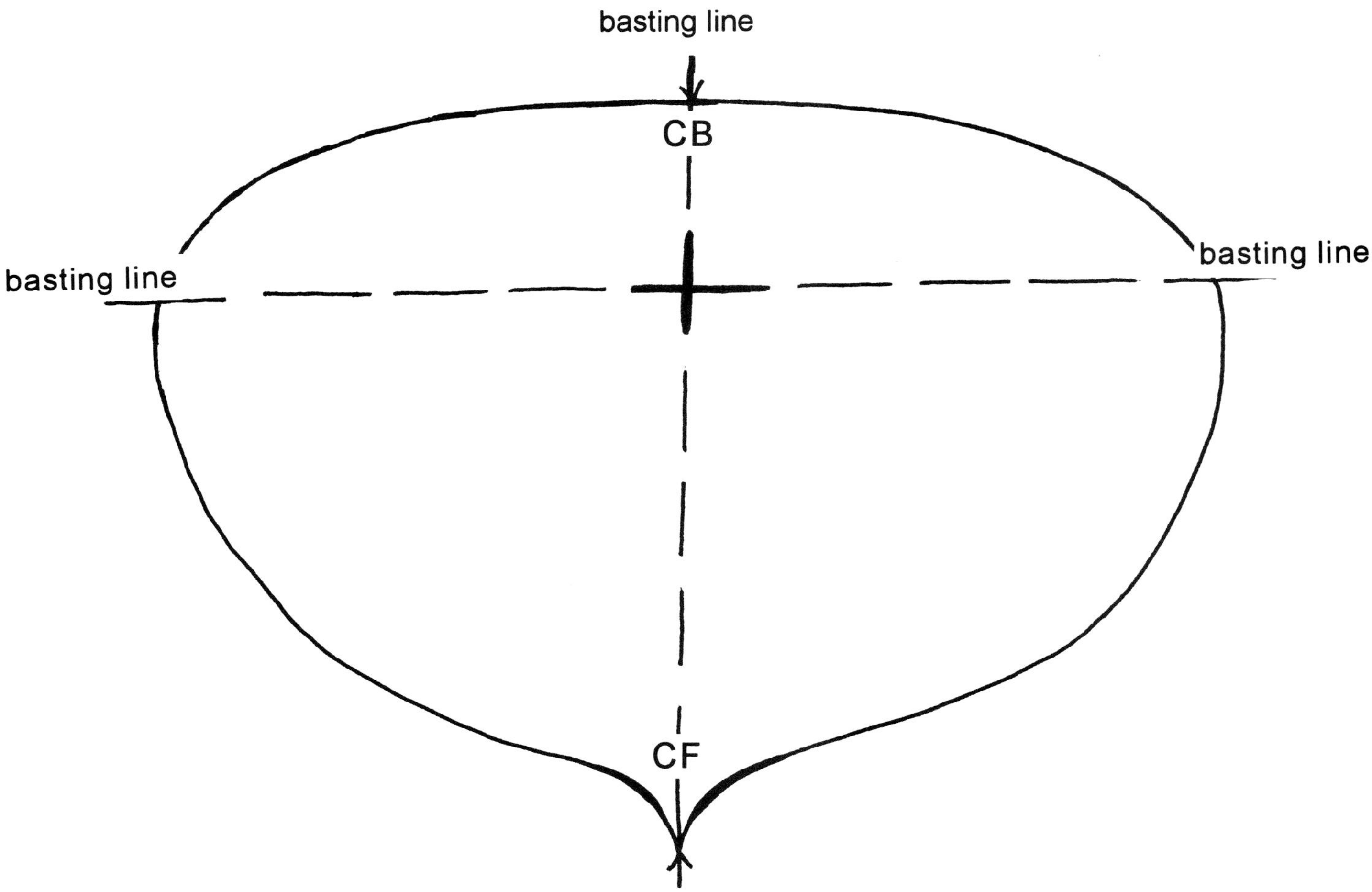

Now slash between every stitched line from the topside leaving the bottom layer intact. This might take rather heavy duty shears, depending on how many layers you have used.

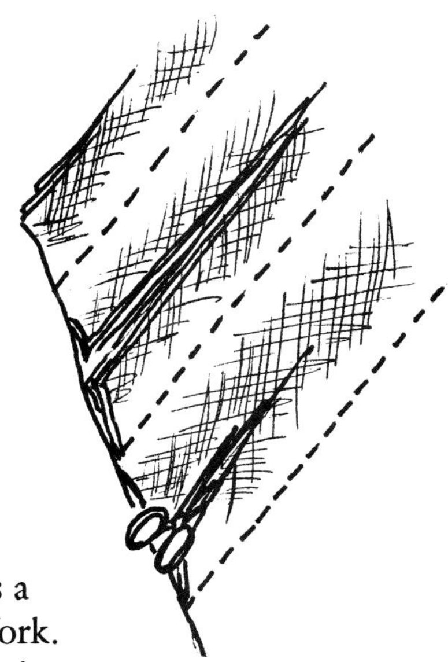

Stitch together the underarm seams, maybe using a serger, maybe machine stitching and binding the raw edges for a more finished look.

Cut a bias binding (explained in chapter 1 if you would like to review), and bind all edges – wrists, neck, fronts and bottom. An alternative if you want the jacket to button would be to put buttons and buttonholes in straight – cut front bands (illustrated middle next page).

Another project shown on this program was a vest by Kathy Smith of Rochester, New York. It was a collage of many types of fabric manipulations. A section of it was treated this same "blooming" way, but with very close rows. They were stitched $^1/_2$" apart making the cut fringe only $^1/_4$" long. This would take sharp points to cut between rows.

My granddaughter's jacket mentioned earlier was a "blooming" flower garden. The "flowers" were stitched in a diamond shape, cut 4 times as shown, and after a few washings they got very fluffy!

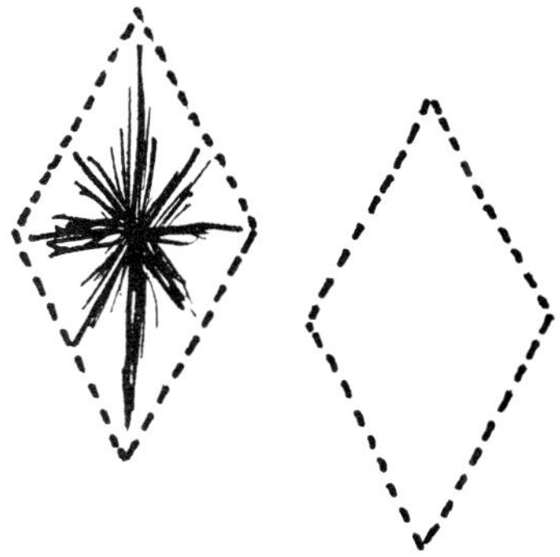

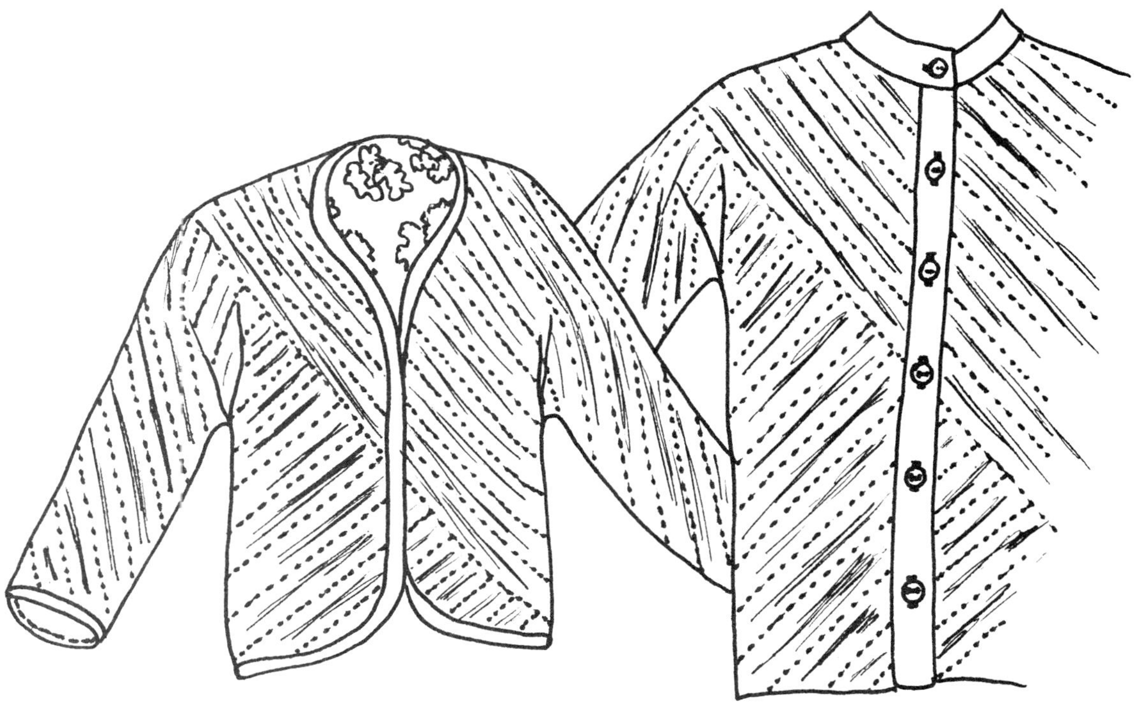

Hidden Assets

Program 8

I marvel at how every sewer looks at a fabric and sees something completely different than what others have seen. Clothing goes in different directions and certainly there is a serious track that leads you to pursue the no-nonsense pure quality, sophisticated look. There's also the flipside where you just have fun manipulating and joining fabrics. Pull out all the stops texturizing and embellishing and see what results.

You have fabrics hidden away that you can no longer like years late. If the basic colors still appeal to you they may be ideal for stitching, wrinkling, pleating, couching cords and ribbons – refabricating. Bring out the hidden assets by enhancing in a variety of ways, and at the same time camouflaging what you do not like. Use any type fabric for this. Because of the manipulations you will probably choose to dry clean it later. Therefore mix anything together without worrying about compatibility.

Several vests were shown on this program because a vest is a small article, quickly completed. A vest is fun sewing as opposed to the "investment dressing" garments that remain in a serious wardrobe year after year without becoming dated. These fun projects may not weather the test of time so wear them a lot right now!

Some of these vests were made by Kathy Smith of Rochester, New York. They ran the gamut of designer manipulation techniques, interestingly pulled together into a small garment. On just one she had:

Pleating: A fabric pleater (can be purchased from Clotilde's notions catalog) is used to tuck your fabric into the pleater's folds, wrong side up. Use any flat thin object to aid in this tucking. A credit card works just fine or that metal pocket former device is another example. After your fabric is tucked in the slots, steam press in place. Cover with a fusible interfacing cut to size and fuse.

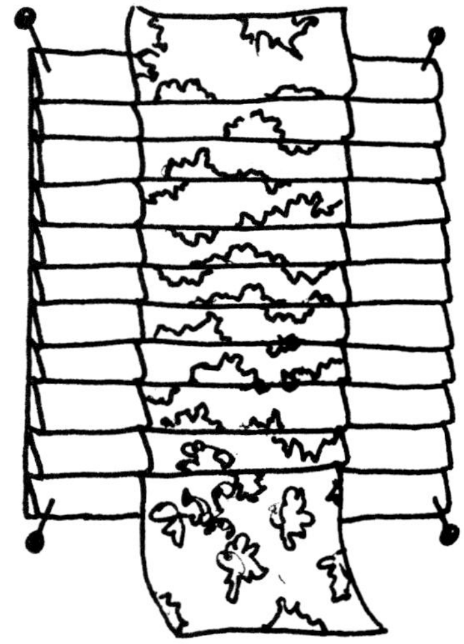

Remove from the pleater by bending it and the pleated fabric rolls out. Leave it as is or further manipulate it by stitching rows across the pleats, alternating directions as the pleats push back and forth.

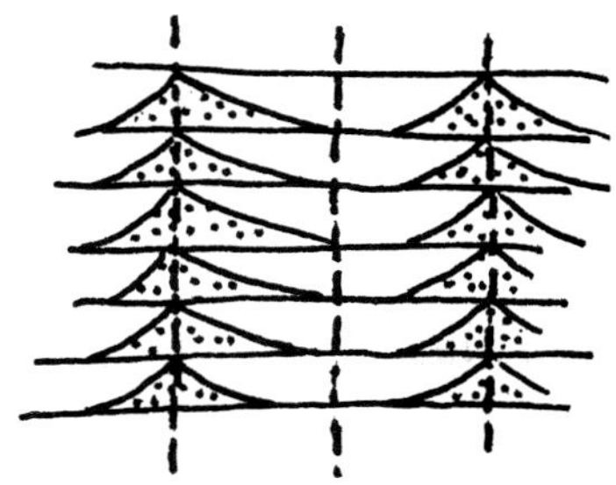

Decorative Stitches: Try out all your machine's possibilities by randomly stitching curvy rows intersecting as they ramble. Do this in a contrasting or metallic thread that really shows up. If doing much stitching, a little reinforcement may be needed on the backside to support all that stitching. This could be permanent support fabric or a tearaway stabilizer. If the metallic thread gives you any trouble (shredding or

breaking), loosen the tension slightly and try a metafil needle. This is made for stitching metallic threads, and any machine dealer carries them.

Lace and Ribbons: Lace strips might cover seam joinings and are especially appealing when ribbons are woven through it.

Stitching Over Ribbons: Narrow ribbons on a solid background really show off the machine's decorative stitches. This is actually couching but a little more elaborately done.

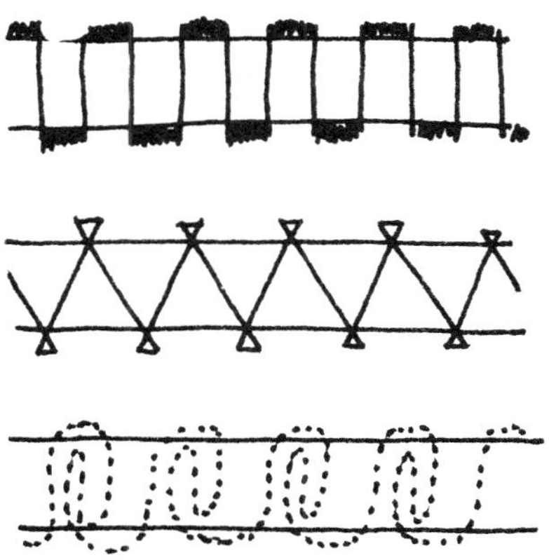

Couching: What we ordinarily think about associated with this term is a simple zigzag stitch to hold cords, braids, yarn, ribbons in place. They can go in straight lines or curvy ones or really, really curvy to form solid blocks. What makes this very easy is a braid foot or cord foot that holds this absolutely in place for accurate stitching. Do this over flat or pre-wrinkled fabric to hold the wrinkles in place against a backing fabric.

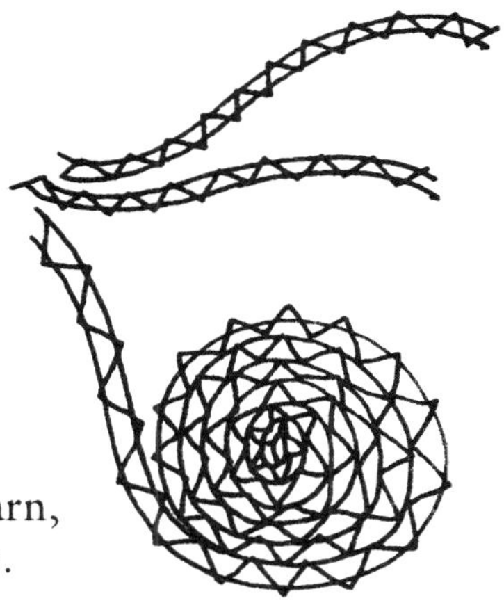

Blooming Rows: Stitch layers of fabric together, then slash all but the bottom layer. This will "bloom" more with each washing or wearing. This is described in depth in the previous program.

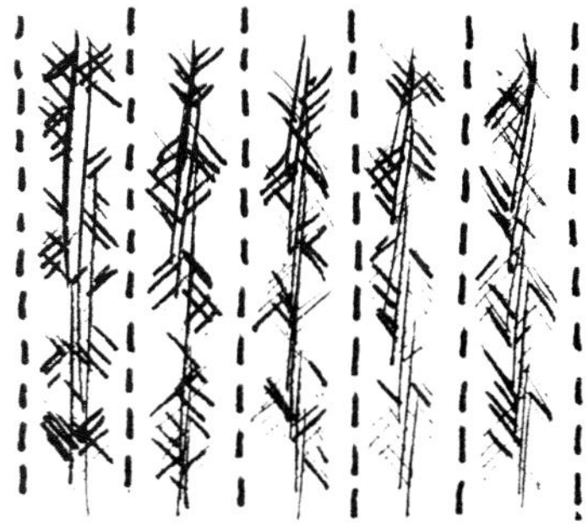

Beads: Purchased by the yard come attached and dangling from a flat braid. This braid is sometimes attractive, but frequently not meant to be seen. In that event, stitch between the seams so only the beads dangle and show. It is often easy to do this with a combination of the zipper foot and a slight change of the needle position to stitch as close to as possible, but avoid hitting the beads.

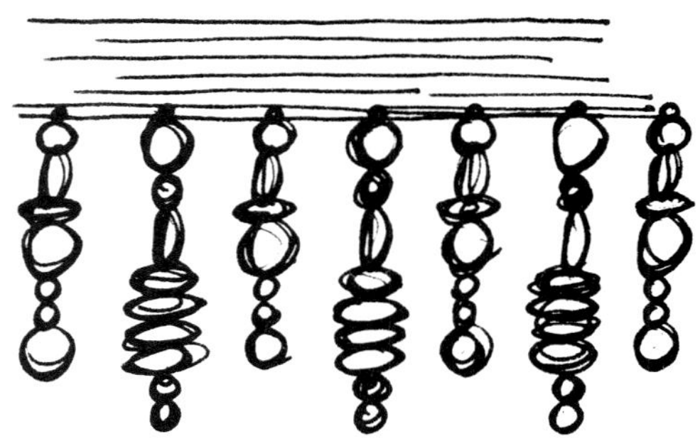

Random Stitching Reversible Fabric: One of Kathy's really neat vests was a combination of coordinated fabrics. One side striped, the other side flowered; try a core layer to beef it up somewhat. Think cotton flannel if fleece would be too much. Cut out the vest larger than the pattern as it will shrink somewhat with all the circular stitching. Put layers back to back together and randomly stitch with the feed dog down and using an embroidery foot, darning foot, or spring needle. This allows free-motion stitching in all directions. This is a good place to use up multi-colors of thread ends or perhaps one or many colors of metallic thread. Remember this will be reversible so

use pretty threads in the bobbin. After covering as completely with thread as you want, put the pattern piece back on and trim the edges down to size.

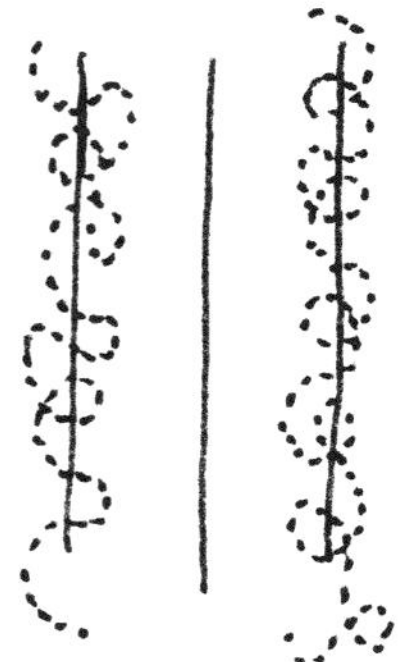

Construct in the usual way, press seams open, and then do more stitching over those edges. ***Or*** overlap at the stitching line and simply do the extra stitching to cover the raw edges. The latter would be flatter since seam allowances are not folded back.

Cut a big stack of 2" fabric squares in a color complimentary to both sides. Fold them diagonally and overlap them somewhat as you go. First stitch all the edges to hold in place. Then go back and cover more thoroughly. A really fun technique, this is something you ought to try.

Something similar I'm doing on a wrinkled silk: This fabric I showed a couple of series ago and sought your ideas about its outcome. It had been wrinkled in the dyeing process. Each little white spot had been tied around a single grain of rice, dipped in the dye, and allowed to dry in that position before being untied. There are thousand of these little spots in that length of fabric. Imagine the work of some person in India!!! These are tiny dots when allowed to wrinkle up. As the fabric is stretched flat the tiny dots grow like flowers blooming in time-lapse photography. To keep it textured, mount on another fabric. That same circular stitching seems to be the best way to lock in the look permanently. Mounted on a light weight cotton for comfortable feel, it will eventually become a garment. Originally I considered fusing a backing on this, but decided against that since it would eliminate some desirable texture. To leave it single layer, it would eventually flatten out and grow too much in size. Mounting and stitching keeps the texture and preserves the space.

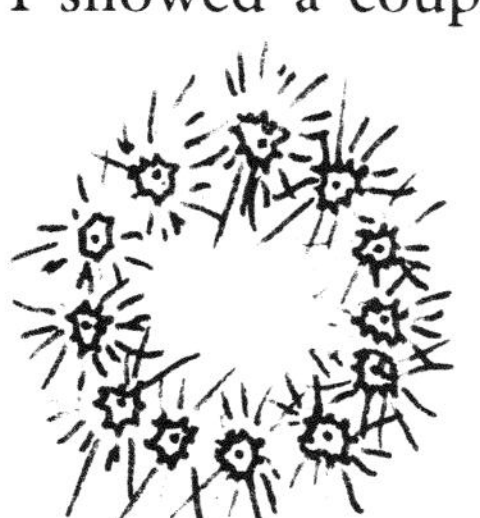

Two vests of mine in many blue-green fabrics are interchangeable between fish print shorts and flower print skirt. The fish print cotton has on the vest back the flat fabric lavishly enhanced by dozens of rows of metallic thread stitching highlighting the fish. The front of the vest fabric was first wet and wrinkled, dried, spread partially out on a knit fusible interfacing and pressed in place to hold the wrinkles permanently. Because of

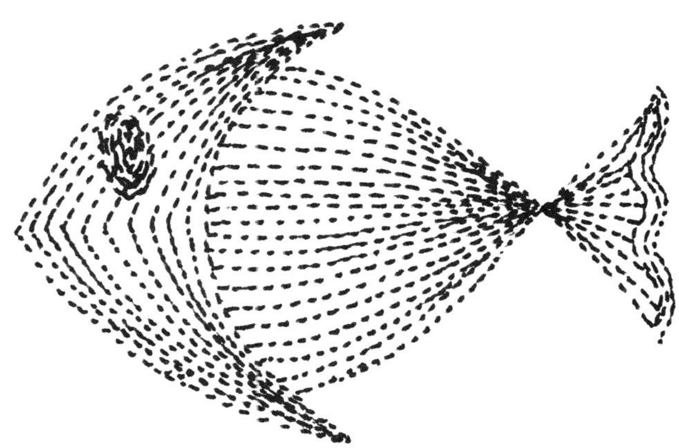

all the fish I decided to emphasize the underwater feeling with lots of wavy seaweed, bubbles, the look of sparkly wetness. Metallic threads in blue, green, and purple were used in great abundance stitching the curvy lines. Metallic cords were couched on for more definitive lines here and there.

The sensible time to do all this elaborate stitching is after it is all fused to the backing and with pattern pieces laid, and cut out. Save your time by stitching the cut pieces only. Unfortunately I was in such a hurry to get to the fun part – the decorative stitching – that I did the whole wrinkled piece ***before*** cutting out the pieces. I refuse to let that effort go to waste now that it's done! I shall use the scraps some way and two projects come to mind. With all the metallic thread it looks more like silk than cotton in its sparkling jewel colors. It would very nicely make an evening bag. Another possibility is to combine with another fabric to supplement, and make it into a large beach bag as is suggested by the fish print.

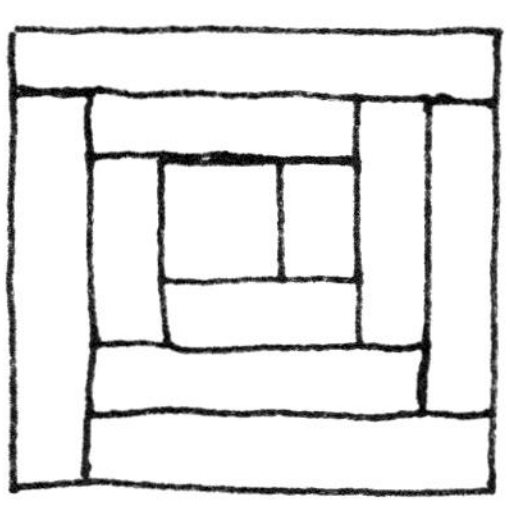

The second vest is log cabin piecing using a few pieces each of the two prints, then combining those with several blue-green, etc., solid color cotton. Usually a log cabin is uniformly cut pieces sewn around and around from the center on out. Design yours however you choose. I elected to combine shapes and sizes starting with one of the two print fabrics in the center of each "cabin".

Pin the center down to a backing, perhaps flannel cut in the pattern shape. Cut the next strip the same length, and as wide or narrow as you like. Edges together, stitch a shallow seam and press out flat.

Move on to the next side and stitch another, press out flat.

It's fine if you're so unorthodox as to add a few to one side before moving on if you feel so moved.

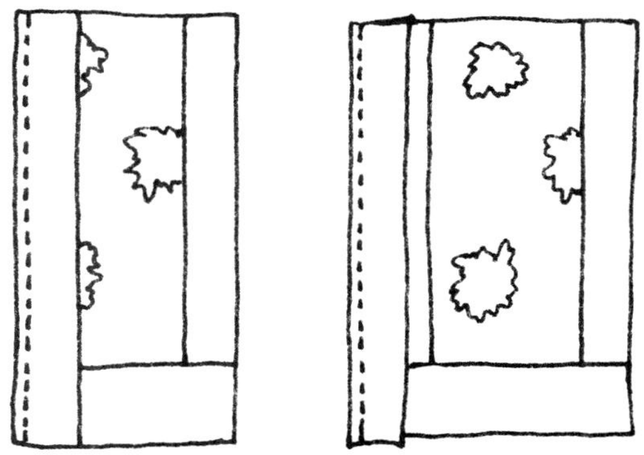

Feel free to create in any way you please. Put these on the diagonal if you'd prefer. Add a few prairie points or some other little accent.What's a prairie point? Fold a rectangle in half. Fold top corners to center.Turn over and stitch all raw edges between two fabrics being joined.

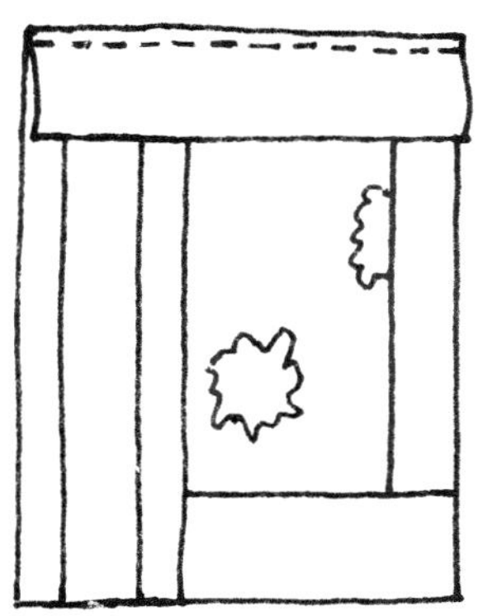

Breaking Away Program 9

When we bought our present house I looked around the empty wide expanses and thought – this is perfect! It's really big and just the right house to fill our needs. By the time we filled it with our belonging, thereby breaking up the spaces, it looked so much smaller.

The same is true of clothing. Adding a seam or other break here and there makes it look smaller and is so easy to do. We'll start with a Bonfit® patterner that can be adjusted in the hips and waist and length so it's exactly right for me. I always make the waistline 1" bigger than I really need it in order to ease it into the waistband and provide for the roundness right under my waist. This is the same reason why expensive ready-to-wear always fits better.

Whether you use an adjustable patterner or a paper pattern, you'll still have to make duplicates in order to cut them up. You'll also have to fine tune them both to accommodate all your personal figure measurements.

Do you have a bit of tummy as opposed to being really flat? If so, better provide some extra height at the center front so that the skirt will hang straight. Are you rounded as opposed to angular and bony right below the waistband? Then stitch the darts in a curved shape rather than in straight lines. Are you kind of straight up and down?

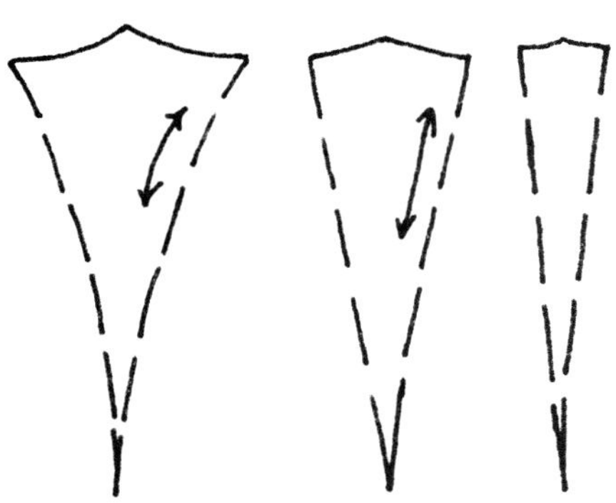

The darts will need to be shallower, or disappear altogether if you're really straight. Does your waistline dip down in back? Also cut down the pattern in the same shape.

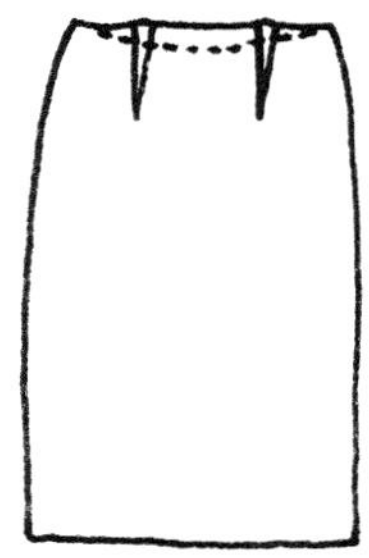

Make these changes in your duplicate pattern so that it completely fits your body as a basic. Then when you add whatever seams extra, it will be strictly design changes, not fitting adjustments.

In a magazine was a photo of a skirt I'd like to have. It was leather and frequently leather garments have many seams because smaller skins make that necessary. No matter what the fabric, I just like the look. Adapt any skirt design from a basic skirt pattern.

The new skirt would have a front panel (for a slimmer look) and the side panels would have horizontal seaming but not at you hips' biggest part. Drop or raise it somewhat. Draw these same lines on the duplicate pattern. Little hash marks help as they later become notches to aid in putting pieces back together.

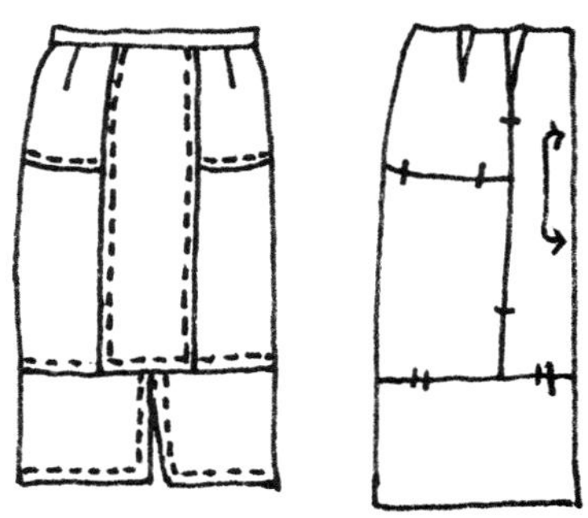

That front panel line is an extension of the center dart. Eliminate the side dart also, if you like, by raising the horizontal line to the point of the dart. That dart is then folded out and taped together. Automatically the waistline becomes curved instead of its former straight line, thus fitting around the curved hip. Draw these lines aided by a yardstick or plastic curve sticks (fashion

rulers) available in notions' departments.

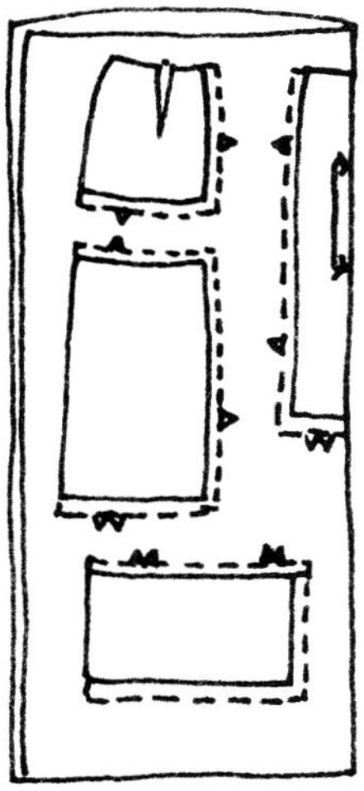

Cut up the duplicate pattern and lay the pieces on fabric allowing for the addition of seam allowances wherever cuts were made. Either mark the $^{5}/_{8}$" seams before cutting or eyeball them if you're good. Remember you only add seams where you've cut. Make notches wherever the hash marks were drawn so it more easily fits together.

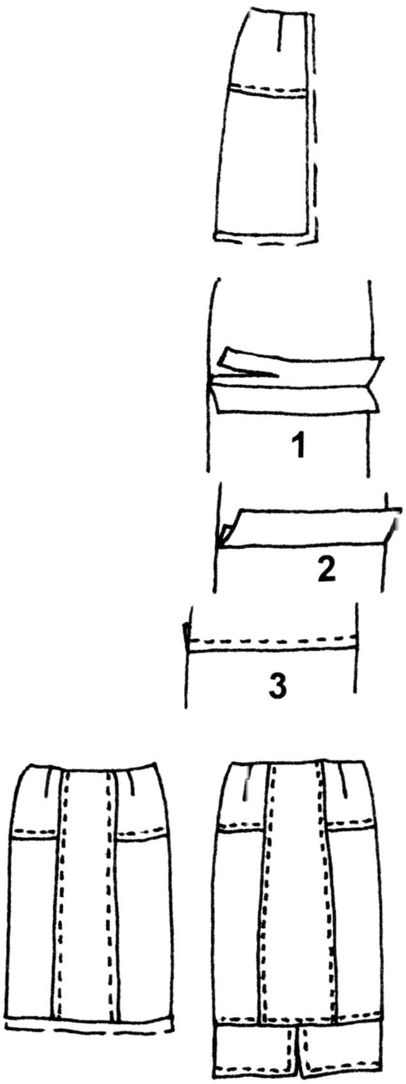

To sew it together think logically how it would work. First would come the side panel dart and horizontal seam. Immediately after pressing that seam open, press it upward, trim the in-between seam allowance and topstitch before joining it to the center panel. Treat that seam the same way. Then add the lower panel and complete the skirt. Notice this is exactly the reverse order of cutting the paper pattern apart.

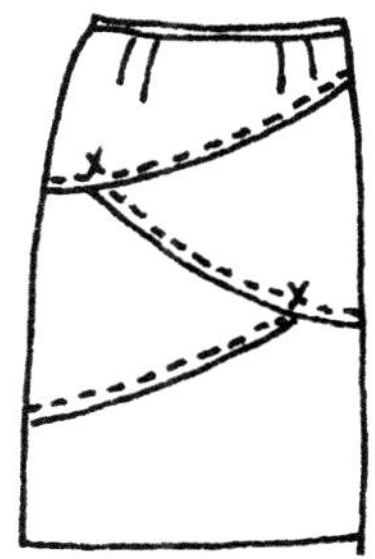

Another skirt was cut into asymmetrical seaming. To do this a whole skirt front pattern will be needed instead of just the half pattern because the left and right sides are different. This off-balance seaming fools the eye and makes you seem a little taller and slimmer. The fact that those lines start narrower than the side seams (note the Xs) further promotes that illusion.

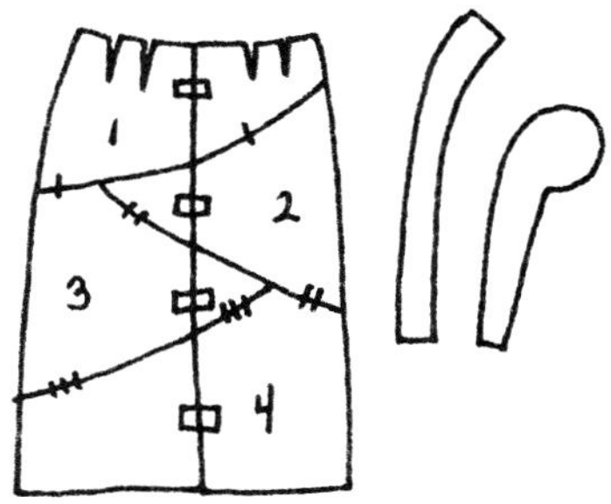

Tape together two duplicate paper fronts. With the aid of a hip curve or a fashion ruler, draw the curved line. When these are cut apart you will need grain arrows to assist in laying the pattern on grain. The center front line can act as this grain line. Add hash marks and number each piece to avoid confusion.

Cut apart, lay on a single thickness of fabric since you only want to cut one of each piece. Again, leave room for seam allowances and when cutting, convert the hash marks to notches. These are especially helpful with the curved lines.

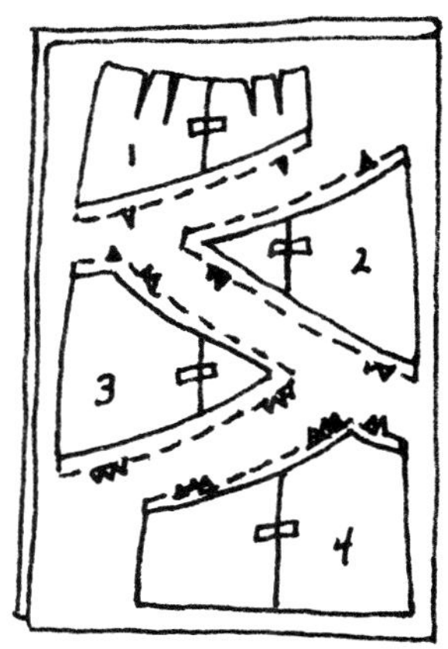

To stitch together, again the reverse order is the only logical way. Pieces **4** and **3** will first be joined. Pin the notches together first with piece **4** on top. This is because **4** has an inside curve that will have to be clipped at intervals so it can open up into little Vs while you pin

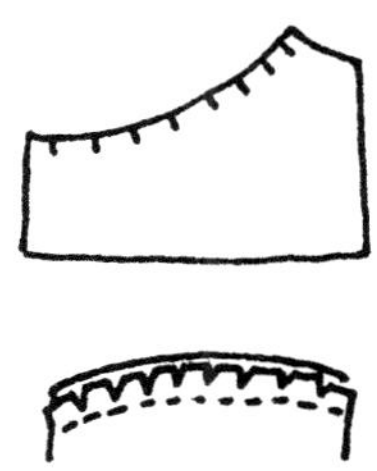

and stitch it to the outside curve of **3**. Press, trim in-between seam, topstitch. Repeat as you join piece **2**, then piece **1**. If you make this in woven fabric instead of leather, you may want to serge the edges of the outside curves. The inside curve with its notched seam need not be finished because it will be the in-between seam allowance, so will be trimmed short before topstitching.

Another skirt made from the same basic pattern had vertical seaming and pockets put in those added seams. Generally when there are two darts in the pattern piece, to make seams of the center darts is more flattering. Because of the pockets, that front panel would be too slim, so outside darts would need to convert to seams instead. This skirt will have gathers so a little extra fullness is added for that.

The pocket addition is easy. When cutting that seamed area, put your hand down on the fabric, fingers spread a little for a generous size, in the position they would go into a pocket. Cut around and you have cut-on in-seam pockets.

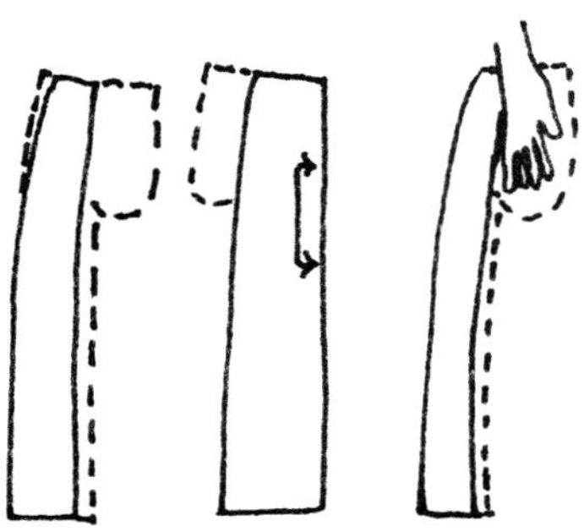

Besides the breaking up of pattern pieces, in this skirt there is also some combining.The skirt back pattern and side front pattern are overlapped at the stitching line. This eliminates the side seam. The upper hip curved outline converts to a dart or gathers.

CB

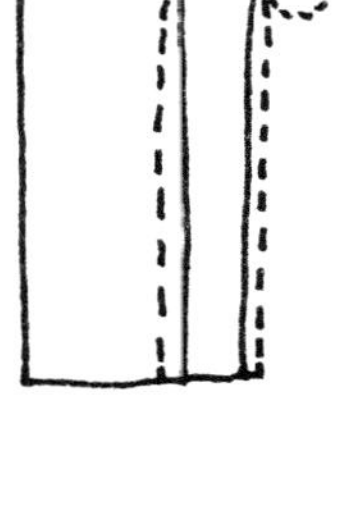

A magenta UltraSuede® skirt is cut the same way as the last example. Instead of turning the darts into gathers, stitch graduated lengths of twin-needle pintucks for the same shape.

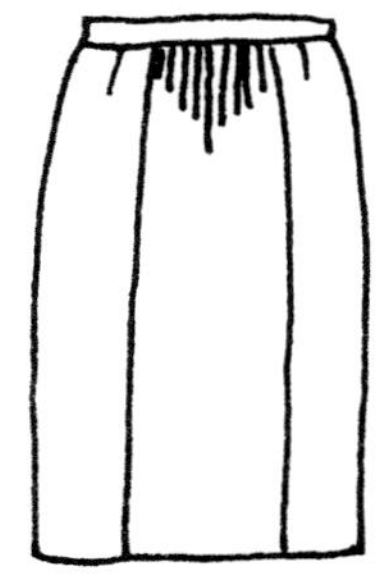

A blue suede skirt from the same pattern takes on a whole different look. The top 2", tapering down to 3" at center front, is cut off the duplicate pattern. This will be a front yoke. Fold out the darts, tape, and the yoke curves, fitting your body without darts. In the lower skirt the remaining small darts convert to slight gathers to stitch onto the yoke. Eliminate the waistband, finish the top edge with a facing.

A skirt is such a simple garment, once you have a basic skirt pattern fine tuned for a perfect fit, you can make any skirt you see from this same pattern. Once you understand how easy it is to change a basic pattern and add other seams, realize you can do the same to a blouse pattern or a jacket pattern, etc. Build on everything you learn by thinking how you can apply this new knowledge to solve a future challenge.

Sometimes rather than cutting extra seams to break up the apparent size of a larger object, think of new possibilities. Pleats will also break size and add some flattering vertical lines to a design.

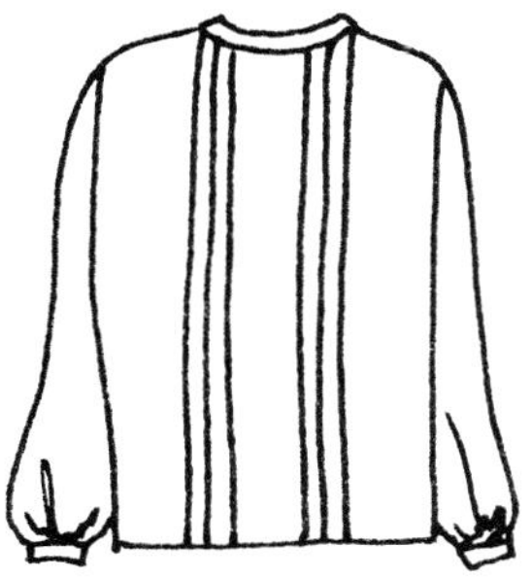

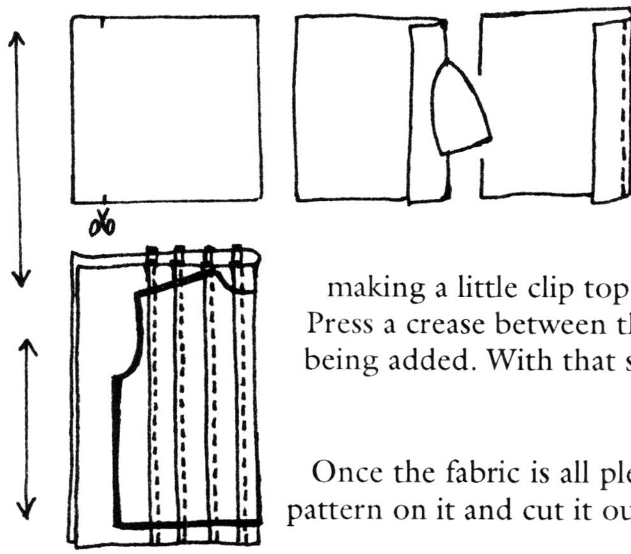

When adding pleats, instead of changing a duplicate pattern, cut a piece of fabric the length of the pattern. Mark and stitch in the pleats. Mark by making a little clip top and bottom in the fabric. Press a crease between the two clips for each pleat being added. With that straight lined fold, stitch a pleat parallel to it.

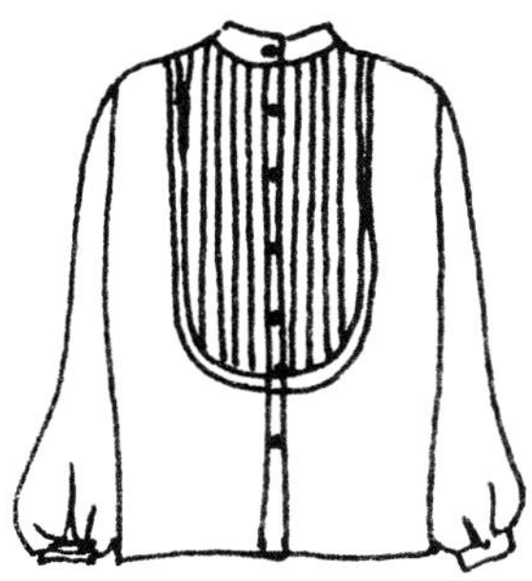

Once the fabric is all pleated, lay the plain, uncut pattern on it and cut it out.

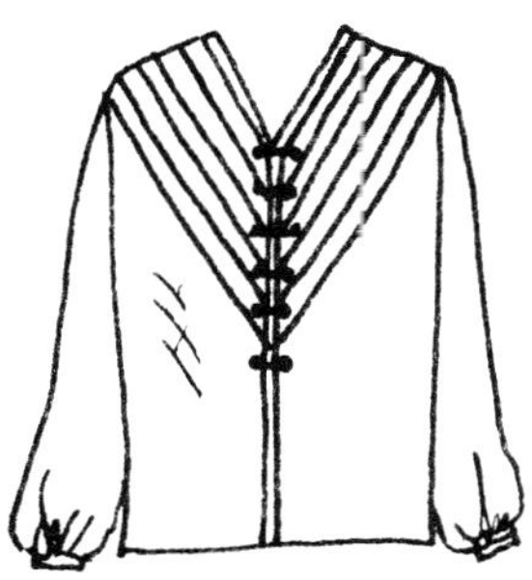

While in Kearney, Nebraska, for a live seminar I saw a very plain, simple jacket on Byrnece Mefferd. Really striking in its unbroken lines and gorgeous color of suede, Byrnece looked wonderful in it. She is a petite person. Picture this on a larger person and the jacket would be less flattering. There's an easy way to break up this big shoulder expanse if the sleeves can be lengthened. Pinch up a flange on the shoulder and topstitch it about 3" or 4" down the front and down the back leaving the rest to fall in a soft pleat. This not only looks narrower, but also squares off the shoulders in case your shoulders are sloping.

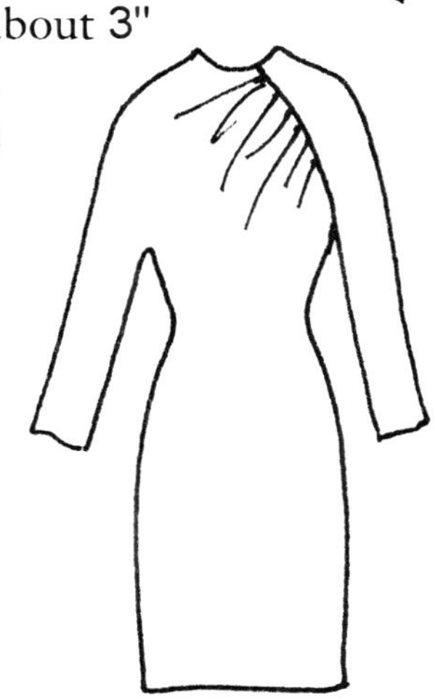

Asymmetrically draped garments also create a smaller optical illusion. A dress draped to one shoulder or a skirt with a sarong drape may be patterns you'd like to try. They can be made from basic patterns, of course. But its also possible to buy such a pattern if you prefer.

Show-Off Sheets Program 10

These are the type sheets that of course make a room look wonderful. So beautifully coordinated you might choose to redecorate; some clever ladies might instead choose to wear them. When they are too spectacular to hide under blankets, why not sew them into something very special?

Who among you hasn't seen Gone With The Wind at least a dozen times? As home sewers you loved it every time when the green velvet draperies went from window to the sweeping gown on Scarlett's back. If Scarlet could, why not you?

The smashing outfit in blue and white Ralph Lauren sheets you see in the photo section was designed by Vona Marengo who is the American Sewing Guild administrator in Worcester, Massachusetts. If, by the way, you're interested in finding out if there is a guild chapter in your area call (503) 772-4059 or write The American Sewing Guild • PO Box 8476 • Medford, OR 97504

This is a great way to connect with other people who have similar interests as you have. It would be great to network with them, and see what programs they have to offer.

Vona made this coat from Folkwear Tibetan Panel Coat #118. Two Ralph Lauren sheets were combined with another fabric, all in identical tones. The first Lauren sheet is a striped with a border print, and the other has a lavish floral design.

Let's first think what kind of yardage you can get from sheets of different sizes. Compare the cost per sheet yardage with the cost per bolt yardage.

Sheet Size	36" yardage	45" yardage	54" yardage
twin	4 3/4 yard	3 3/4 yard	3 1/4 yard
double	6	4 3/4 yard	4
queen	7	5 2/3	4 3/4
king	8 1/2	6 3/4	5 3/4
pillowcase	1	3/4	2/3

Let us also consider how much border width is in each size and do a cost comparison of one particular sheet.

Sheet Size	Inches Wide	Yards of Border	Price
twin	66"	almost 2 yards	$15
double	81"	over 2 yards	$35
queen	90"	2 1/2 yards	$50
king	109"	3 yards	$65
pillowcase	38" x 2	just over 1 yard x 2	$35

You might look at a designer sheet and think $65 for one sheet is rather expensive. At first glance it seems like a lot but that king size sheet gives you close to seven yards of fabric. That breaks down to a little over $9 per yard of 45" fabric. Not a bad price; you can often find them on sale for much less.

Remember the borders, however. You know that a flat sheet will have a border on only one end. If it's mainly border you're after, look on this chart at how many inches you will get per sheet. The twin is almost two yards wide for $15. The king is three yards for $65; over four times as much money. For that one extra yard, you have spent $50! If you don't **need** the border in one piece, get two or more twin sheets. You don't always have this BIG a difference in price ($15 – $65) between sizes, but you definitely need to think it through.

How I would approach this planning at home is to first spread out on a big floor space a sheet of whatever size you have. Lay out your pattern pieces on top and shuffle them around until you get the best arrangement. Even if this is a solid color or a white sheet, you know the border would be on the top hem so you could plan accordingly. Decide if your pieces fit best on two twin sheets, one king – or exactly what is the best alternative.

If your yardage needs are different from the sheet size you're are experimenting on, figure that in your calculations. At least if you can physically lay out the pieces in advance, you know what to expect and the job will be easier for having pre-thought it out.

We tend to think about using fabrics in as large a piece as possible – the entire pattern piece cut as one. This isn't the only way. Vona mixed the striped sheet, a flower-dragon Oriental print, and some yard goods in like colors. Be aware that a lot of breaking up is a powerful option. A distinct possibility is appliquéing some specimen area of a print to a different background.

The coat inside is also quite wonderful and not just one piece of lining fabric. It is a combination of all the fabrics. Embroidered in English are translations of the Chinese characters on the outside.

This showpiece involved more hours than anyone could imagine! I was so relieved when it was safely back in Vona's hands! This was one of those garments that had nothing to do with need – unless it was the need for self-expression, the need to create something unique and beautiful, the need for a concrete display of inner thoughts and feelings.

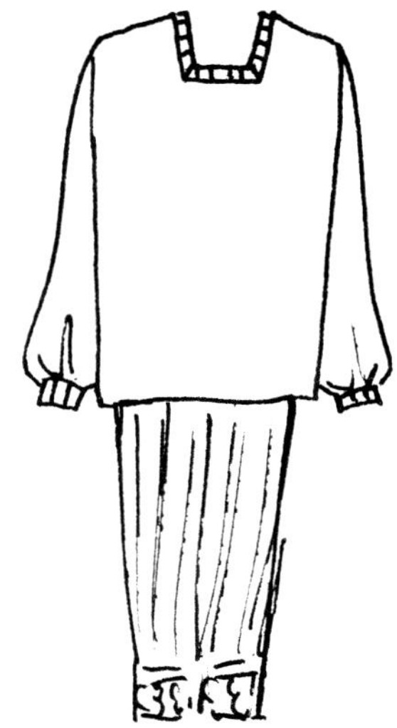

Under the coat is a pant outfit. The overblouse is white cotton, the square neckline bound in the striped sheet. The pants, created using the striped sheet, have an elasticized waist; the border accents the ankles of tapered legs.

Ralph Lauren was behind another coat shown on this program. A blanket with native American designs challenged Fred Bloebaum of California to invest the necessary thought in planning. How best to arrange the pattern pieces on the blanket designs? Pricey items – you have only one chance to do it right!

The weight of one of these blankets plus the fact that both sides are beautiful prompted Fred to make a one-layer coat unobstructed and unencumbered by facings, interfacings, and linings. All the seams are beautifully finished in self-fabric. If straight lined, a flat-felled technique works well. If curved it may be necessary to cover with a separate strip.

The collar is quite large so one layer here was the ideal way to handle it. Fred was careful

to lay the pattern so that designs would be in the most flattering areas, running the most flattering direction. For example, long vertical designs are lengthwise on the coat. A horizontal border is at the hemline. The sleeve design is diagonal indicating raglan sleeves at about this slant.

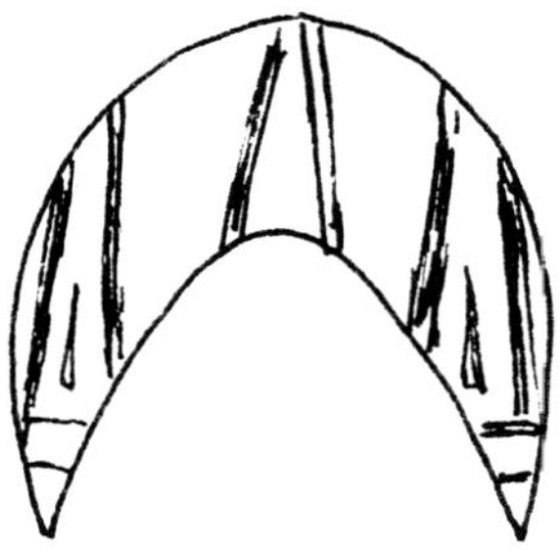

The collar direction could run whichever way the remaining blanket space dictates. For example, if cut with design sideways, it would run more with the shoulder slant. If cut lengthwise with the grain on the center back, it would end up in more of a V slant.

The entire edge is bound with a $1\frac{1}{2}$" strip of leather folded in half. A vintage large button fastened by a leather loop accents perfectly.

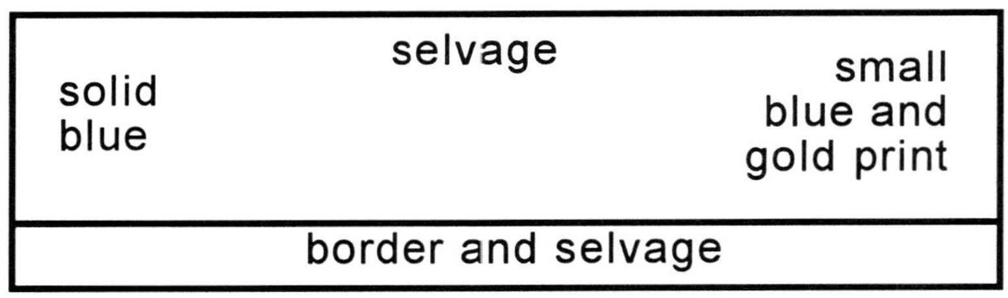

Out of the bedroom but still involving a large piece of fabric with border designs was an Indian sari. This cotton was arranged in an unusual way that required a lot of thought. Suzanne Klemenz of Louisville, Kentucky, elected to fashion this into a suit. From the small print area she made the jacket body and sleeves. Cuffs and collar, continuing around to the facing, are cut from the border. The skirt is the solid navy with some border at the hem. The lining is no less interesting as most of it is the deep navy solid with border being used in a large strip at the inside hem. This fascinates me; I find more and more in pricey wearable art shops that a great deal of interest goes into the lining. It's a pleasant surprise when your lining is very special; possibly a little secret that only you know. But if you take it off and lean it over the chair you occupy, the whole world knows you have an out-of-the-ordinary garment.

Whether you finish with the border at the top or the bottom in horizontal stripes, somewhere used vertically, or perhaps even cut on a diagonal, make no hasty decisions. Use it outside the garment, inside as a hidden treasure, or break it up to combine with other fabrics. Make this thoughtful piece good for the long haul to be sure you get out of it your time, effort, talent's worth!

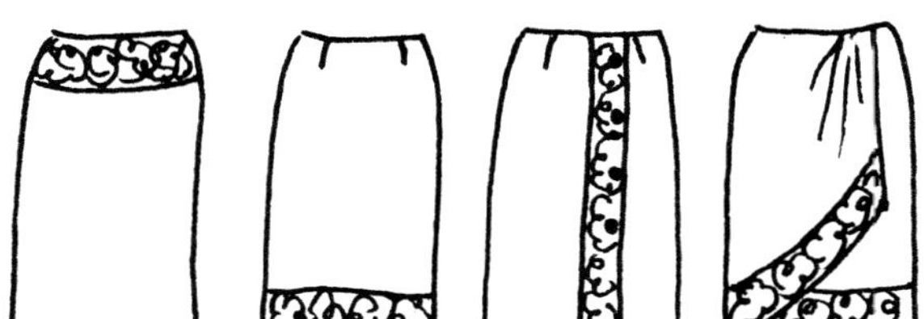

The following page diagrams the techniques and placement of fabrics on Vona's spectacular coat.

Front

- Heavily stuffed trapunto dragon and flowers appliquéed on striped background
- Textured yard goods
- Dangle tear drop pearls
- Triangluar log cabin piecing in several prints
- Silver quilting stitches
- Hand beaded Chinese characters

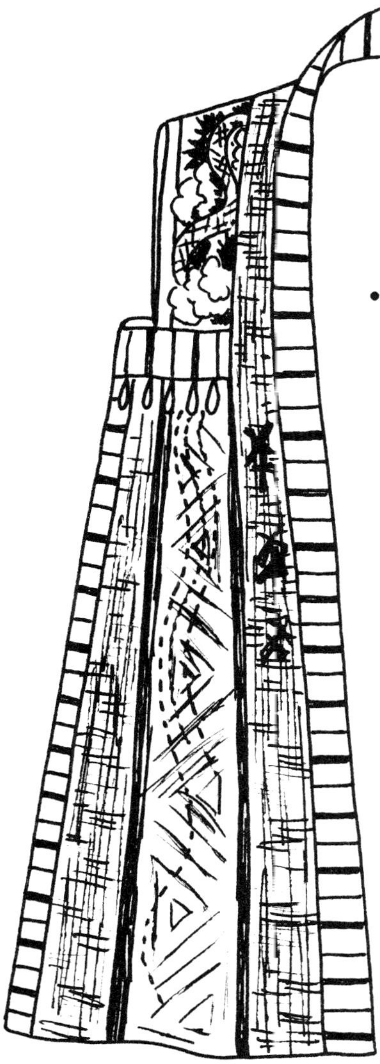

- all panels flared at bottom for a more graceful drape

Embroidered inside the hem is
"Be as lucky as you desire"
– words of wisdom

Back

- Appliqué of trapunto flower print
- More hand beaded characters that translate to lovely words such as peace, harmony, butterfly, flowers, beauty – insight into Vona's inner being.

Simply Wonderful Program 11

Two series ago we "created" a 4000 year old coat that is just as fashionable today – the bog coat. I just cut and folded to produce a garment all in one piece with no waste. Make this in any fabric – it will always be elegant!

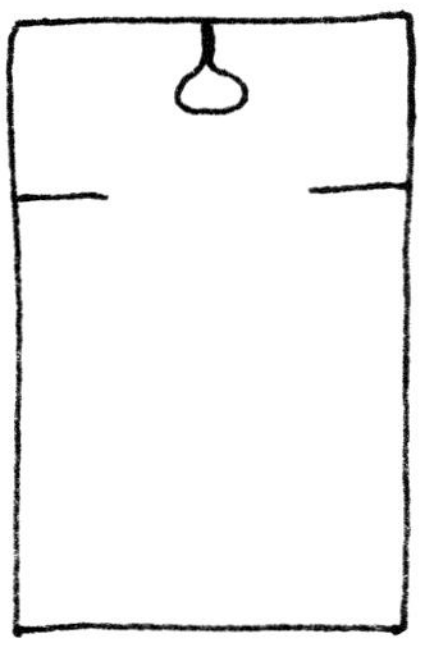

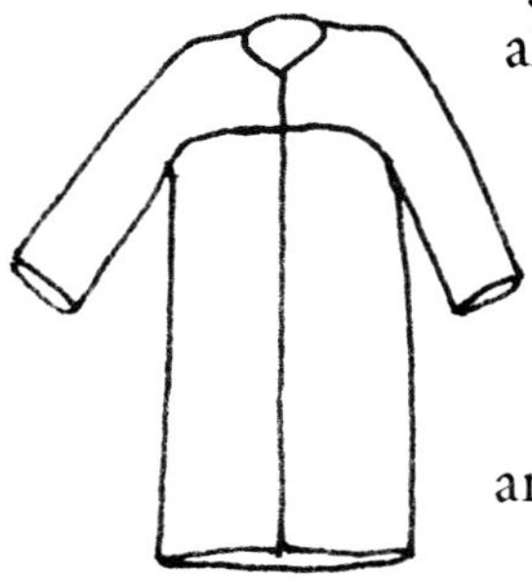

We travel frequently presenting live seminars, and I always make time to visit wearable art shops from California to Florida to Maine. While marvelling at the ingenuity of these artists, I am also inspired.

I spied a coat as appealing as the bog and of a like age. So many of these are produced in Nepal and Tibet that it seems to be a Himalayan concept. The body is merely a rectangle, pleated into flanges on the shoulder to give it overall shape. A lower band reins in the fullness in the hip area. Large sleeves fill the whole side and taper to a slim wrist. This was the starting place, only slightly modified on the program.

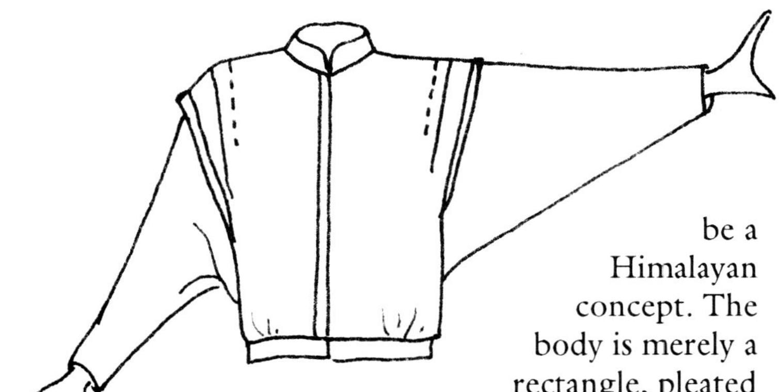

Basic pattern for the jacket body illustrated right. This "one size fits most" pattern covers sizes 8 to 16, but you can easily make it smaller or larger. Notice it's about twice as long as it is wide.

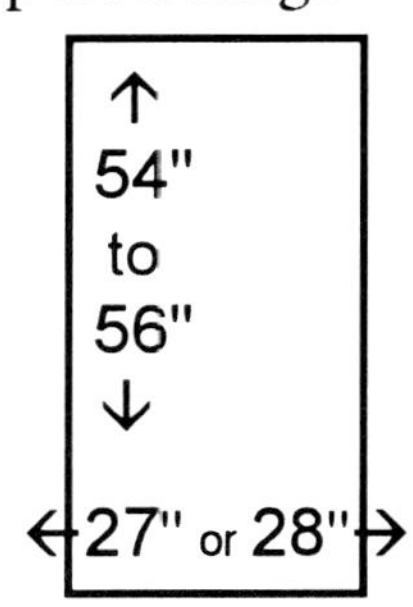

Make this in any fabric, light, heavy, or somewhere in between. I've made them in thick wool melton, man-made leather, and washed rayon. A silk one with organdy ribbons is in process. Use polar fleece, linen, upholstery fabric, knits – anything you fancy.

Here's how that works up into a jacket: Add front bands, armscye bands, collar, side seams, sleeves, lower band, pockets, shoulder flanges, fasteners – you're finished. Shall we discuss that in more explicit detail?

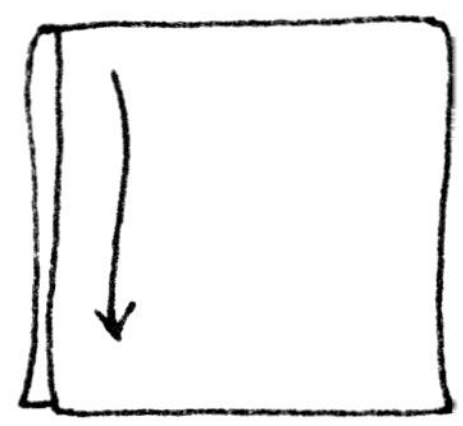

fold in half to find shoulders

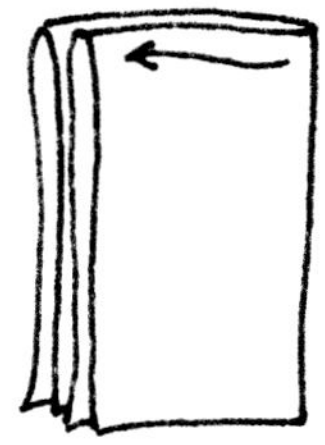

fold sideways to find center front and back

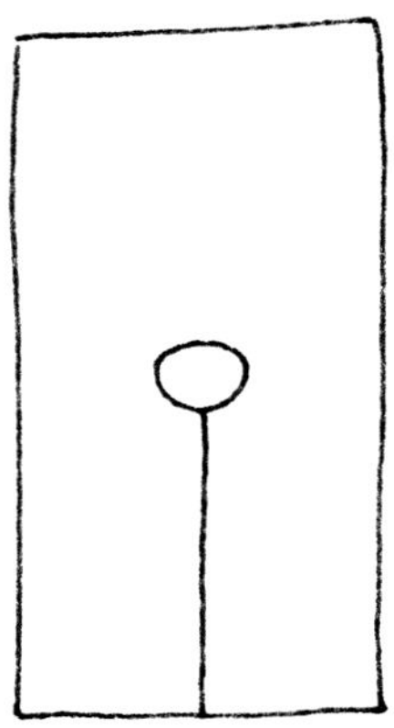

cut front and neckline

The layout for 2 yards of 54" fabric is at the top of next page. There is nothing sacred about these measurements so change them if necessary. This jacket was meant to cover your bottom and be worn with pants, but shorten it to waist length if you like.

A layout for 45" fabric would require $2^{1}/_{2}$" yards. If using a one-way fabric, you will need extra to cut the sleeves the same direction.

If you are lining the jacket, cut it exactly the same except none of the bands will be needed in the lining fabric.

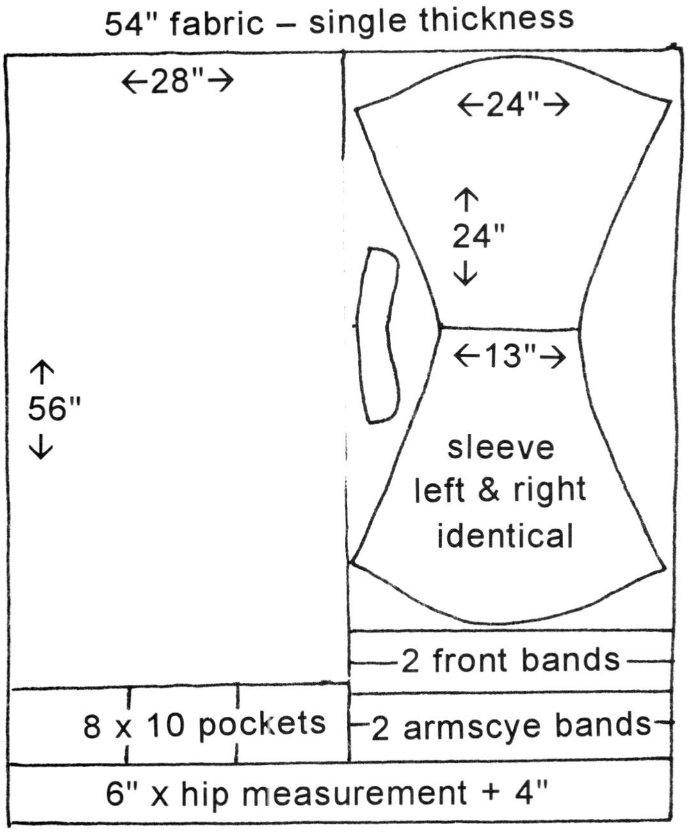

All the straight pieces with their dimensions are obvious. Where did the sleeve and collar pattern come from? I offer two solutions:

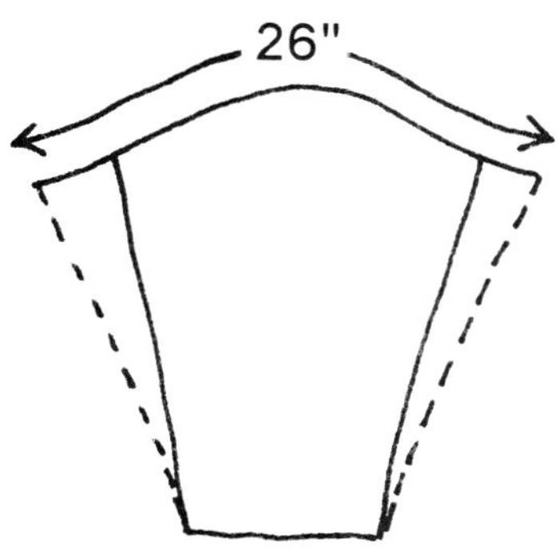

A: Borrow a sleeve pattern from any coat or jacket pattern, and simply widen the underarm points until they are 26".

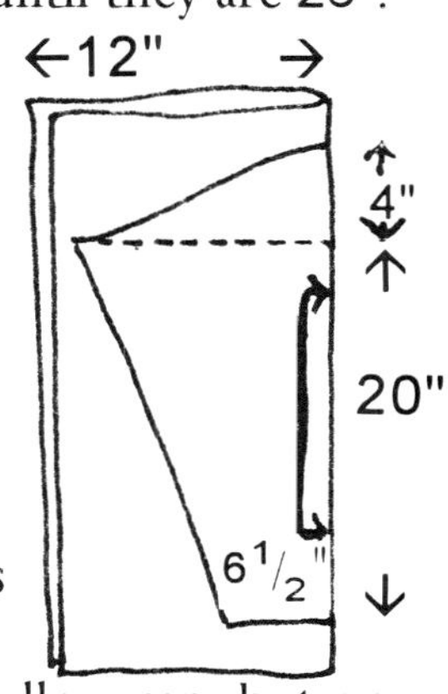

B: Draft your own pattern on folded paper like this. From the fold line at the top make a dot. Measure down 4" and make another dot. Measure down 20" – this is the lower edge. Connect lines as shown. This is a shallow cap, but on this casual jacket it works because the shoulders drop somewhat. The two sleeves are identical back and front.

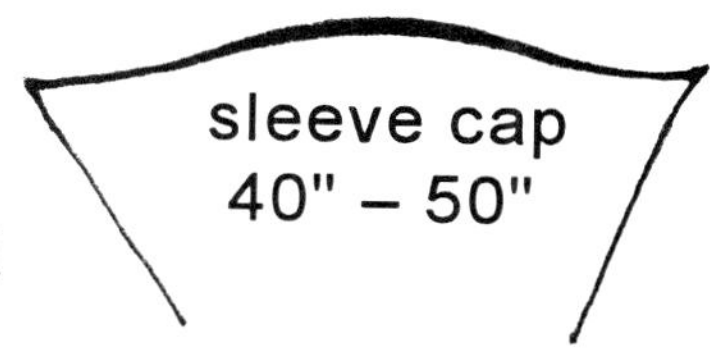

These sleeves are narrowed considerably more than those sketched at the beginning of this chapter. To be so low cut in the armscye would take a lot more fabric than these and be too bulky in the heavy melton.

Collar pattern is on last page of chapter

If you plan on embellishing, now is the time – as soon as everything is cut out. A jacket loaned from Louise Mensing, Virginia, was of matte silk noil implemented by shiny silk charmeuse appliqués – just beautiful! Suggestions for such additions in chapter 12.

If the jacket will remain unadorned, proceed with construction. Fold the lining rectangle in fourths and lightly press the folds to mark locations. Align the jacket rectangle and the lining, back to back. Pin securely all around the outer edge and up the center front.

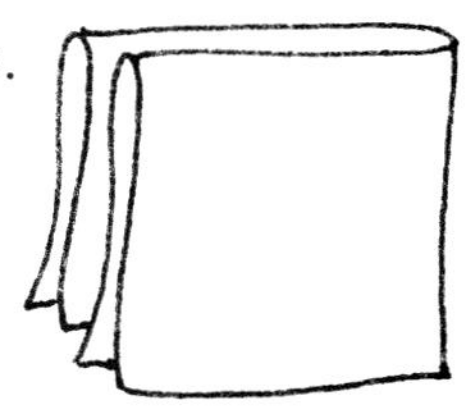

Make a tracing of the neck template and pin in place on the lining, aligning the shoulder points with the horizontal crease and **CB** and **CF** with the vertical crease.

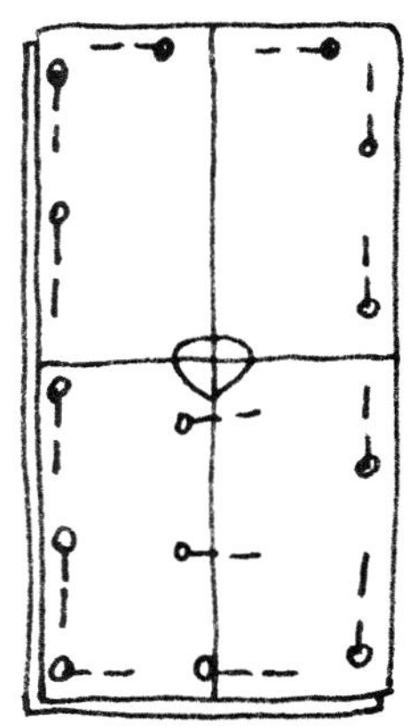

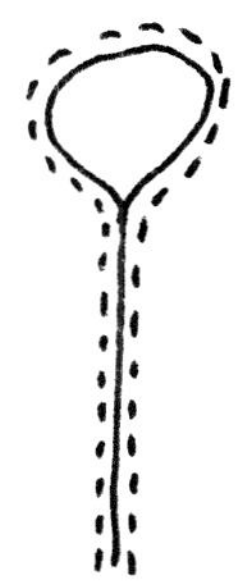

Staystitch all around the outer edge, up the center front (**CF**) in two lines about $^{1}/_{2}$" apart so that you can later slash between them, and right at the edge of the neck template.

Now cut up the center front, and after removing the template pattern, cut out the neckline just inside your staystitching, illustrated above, diagram right.

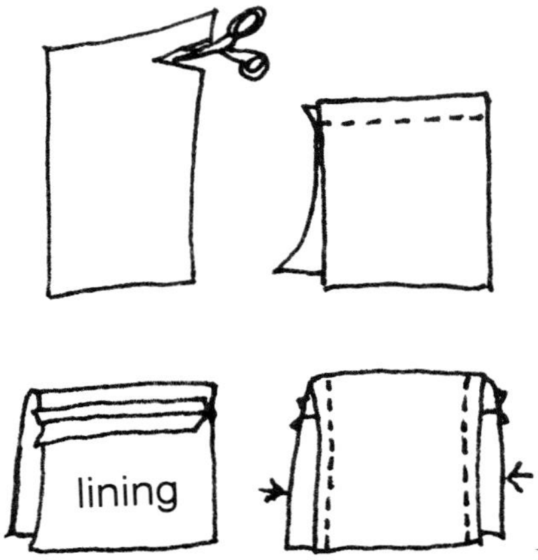

To make the patch pockets, right sides together stitch the upper pocket edge. Press it out flat, seam allowances toward lining. Trim 1" off lining end.

Fold the pocket in half, right sides together. The fashion fabric will extend $^{1}/_{2}$" around to the lining side. When you pin, pull the lining side edges out beyond the fashion fabric. Leave the bottom open. Turn right side out after stitching shallow seams (so you need not bother to trim seams). Because the lining is made smaller, it won't show at the edges. Press flat.

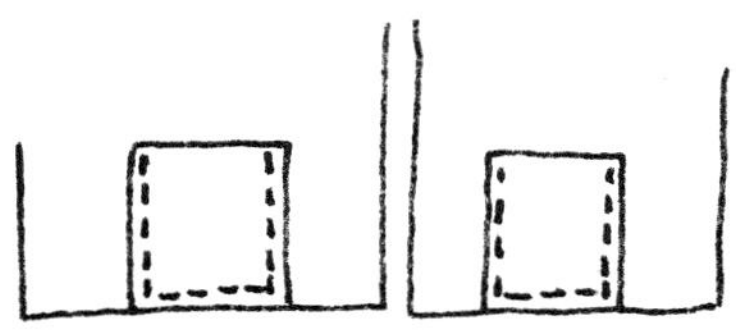

Position pockets 2" or 3" from center front edge and all the way on the lower edge of jacket. Stitch in place.

Decide at this time how the jacket will fasten. The added front bands may later have machine sewn buttonholes and buttons. If you'd prefer button loops, add them now. Cut fabric tubes 1 – 1$^{1}/_{2}$" wide, length dependent on button size. Usually 2" – 3" long for each loop. Stitch this tube as wide or narrow as seems suitable for your fabric weight. Trim seams if they are excessive, and turn right side out with a tube turner. Machine baste in place on jacket right side.

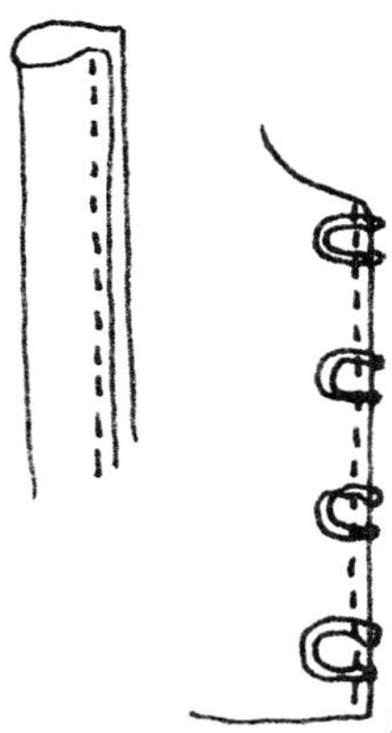

Now is the time to insert tubes on the left side – if you so desire them. Some choices here are a tube with a simple knot tied at its center, a metal antique foreign coin for a button. Use a fabric loop to hold it. A more elaborate Chinese ball was detailed in book 10 so we won't repeat it here. Experiment with wood, bone, or plastic toggles. If these will be attached by a fabric tube, affix now.

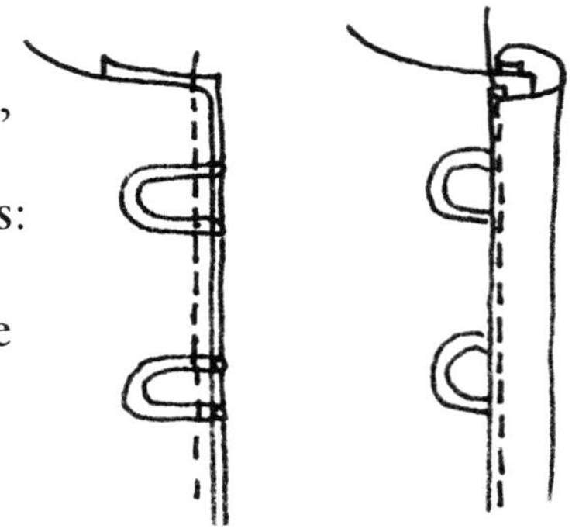

To sew the front band on this, consider either of these two methods: Method (**1**): Put the band right side against the jacket wrong side, and stitch a shallow seam. Turn the strip edge under, bring it around to the garment front so it is a little **wider** than the back seam. Topstitch it down.

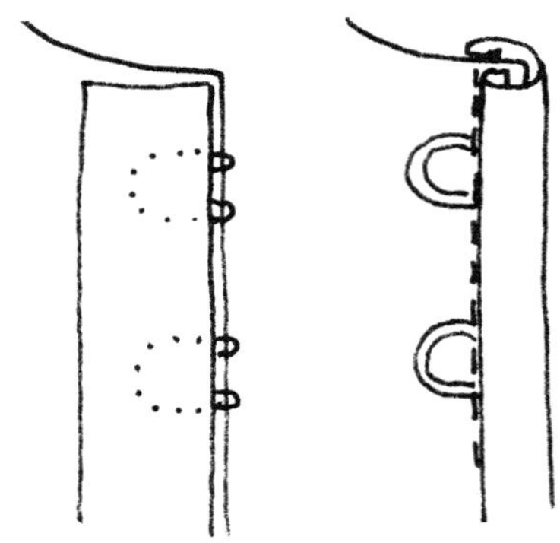

Method (**2**): the opposite in that you begin on top with right sides together and stitch. Fold the band to the backside so it's a little wider than the front. No stitching would show as you stitch-in-the-ditch from the topside, catching the underneath band fold. To eliminate the bulk of heavy fabrics, cut the band on the selvage, and use on the backside instead of the fold.

Interface this band if you prefer a flat band or if machine buttonholes will be stitched. If a puffy look would enhance, tuck in a little strip of quilt batting before stitching the second side.

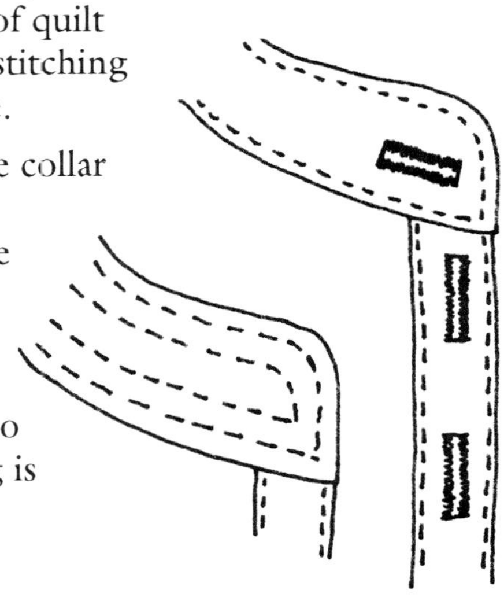

Attach the collar last, and in the same way as the front band. Topstitch if it will show, or ditch stitch if no visible stitching is desired.

The lining side of the collar might also be pad stitched over quilt batting before attaching. Try a trapunto look on the outside, stitching through all padded layers.

Next, stitch up the side seams leaving 25" open at shoulder for the set-in sleeve. If using a thin fabric you might sew French seams. First stitch a shallow seam to the outside. Press flat, press to inside. Stitch a second seam enclosing the short raw edges. Clip at the top of your stitching line to free armscye seam allowances.

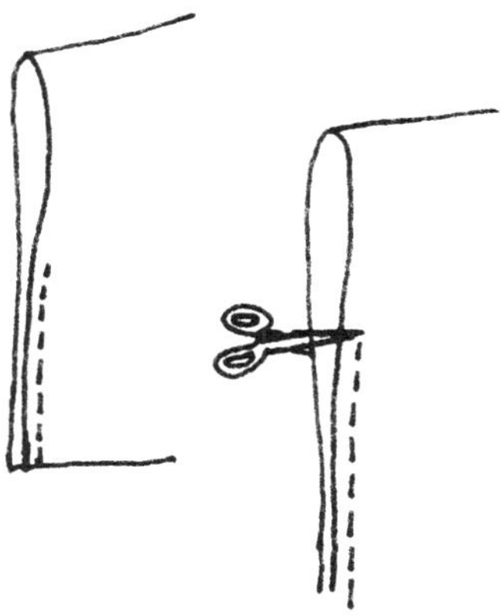

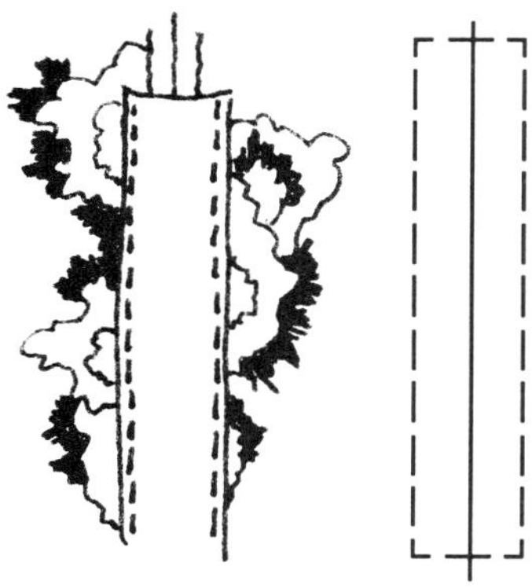

inside outside

If this is a heavy fabric, stitch a single seam right sides together. Press open, trim short , topstitch a ribbon or a bias lining strip over it. Another way would be to leave one lining seam long, trim all others short, fold that over raw edges for a flat-felled seam.

Stitch the sleeve bands into rings, and press seams open. Use these to bind the armscye edges the same as you bound the front jacket edges.

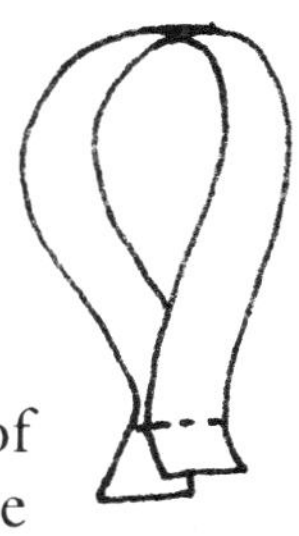

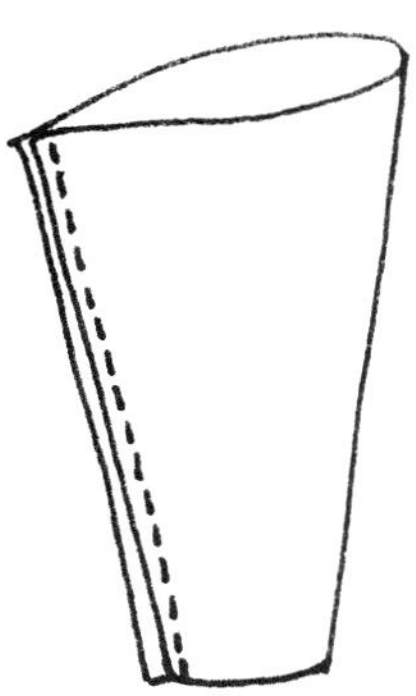

Sew the side seams of the sleeves and sleeve linings separately, right sides together. Press seams open. Right sides together, insert lining inside sleeve and stitch armscye edges together. Press the seam open, turn right side out, and press edge flat.

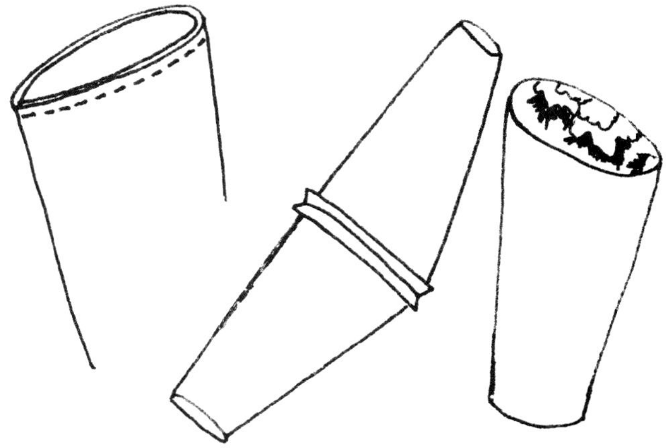

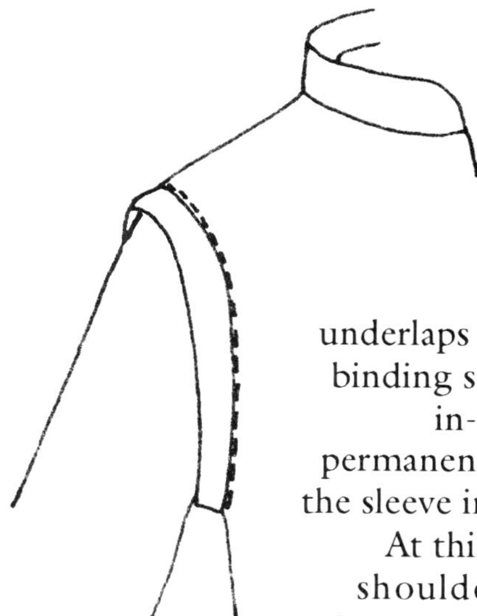

Pin this inside the armscye so that it just barely underlaps the armscye binding seam. Stitch-in-the-ditch to permanently topstitch the sleeve in the jacket. At this point, the shoulders are wide because the shoulder flange (pleat) has not been formed.

A completely different sleeve treatment would give you a one-of-a-kind designer look: zip out sleeves! A jacket to vest conversion requires a slight different construction order so refer to program 13 for information.

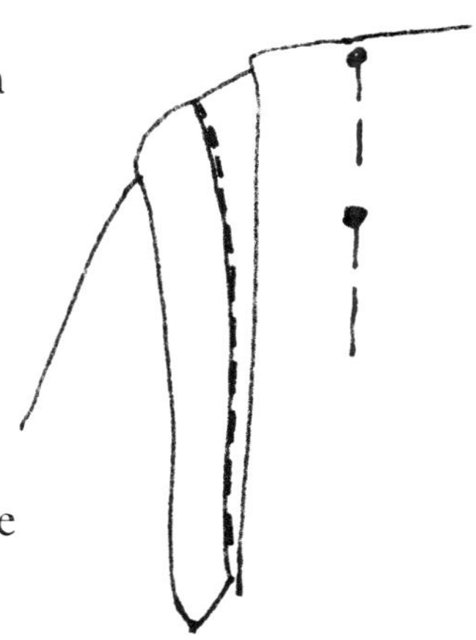

Try on the jacket and pinch up a large pleat or two on each shoulder until you like the look. Tuck in a shoulder pad for a better drape; to somewhat square off your shoulders. This flange will bring the shoulders up into position, only slightly dropped beyond the shoulder-point. This also will furnish a pleat that drapes flatteringly in the bust area.

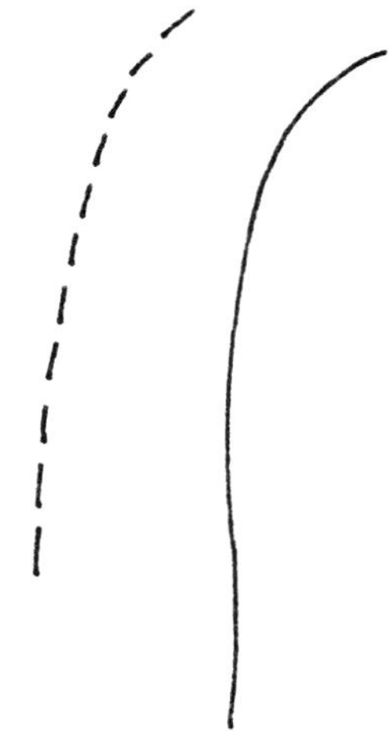

Stitch this flange making sure the lining is flat inside the jacket layer. You will actually be stitching through 4 layers of fabric here, through this big fabric fold. The sleeve will be tucked inside, out of the way. The stitching lines on my jackets are about 10" long, 5" extending each into the jacket front and back. The pleat itself is 2" deep incorporating 4" of fabric. These dimensions can vary as you prefer.

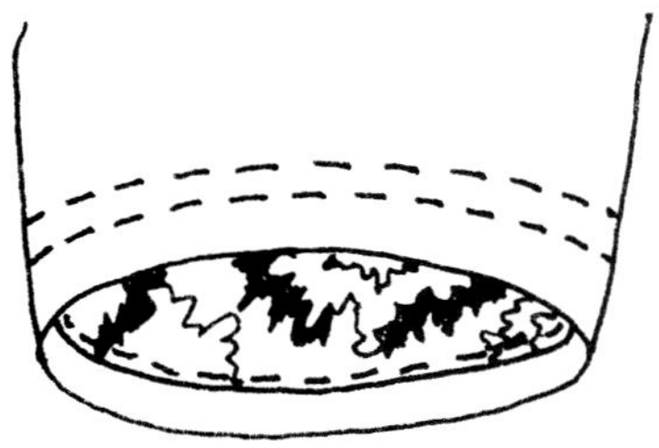

If using shoulder pads, cover with the lining fabric and stitch in place. Now try it on again to pin up the sleeves the preferred length. Not much of a hem was planned for here. It was really meant to be just a generous seam to turn up – perhaps 1" – and press in place. Turn up the lining the same amount or even a little less but ***don't attach it at the sleeve edge***. You need some ease in that lining length so it won't pull up the outer sleeve in an unsightly way. Instead ease it up $\frac{1}{2}$" or more higher than the sleeve edge as long as it covers the raw fabric edge. Pin in place and stitch one or two rows of topstitching.

All that remains is the lower band in the hip area. At whatever level it will hit on your body, decide how loose you prefer that it be. The possibilities are a rather straight or even slightly flared jacket by having this band stitched flat on the lower jacket edge. It would flare a little because of the pinched-in shoulders.

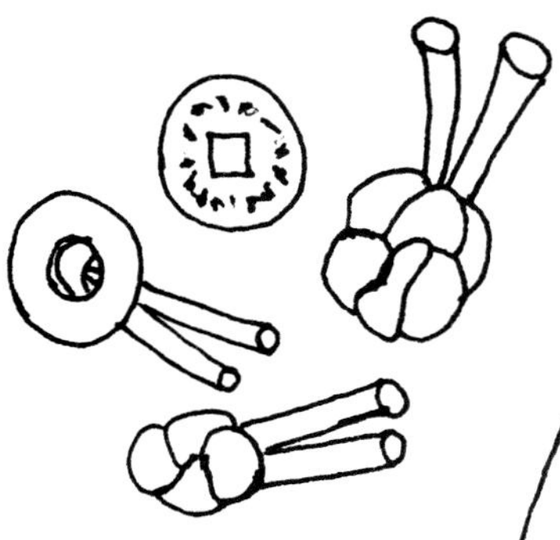

The other possibility is to bring it in closer to the body by making it as short as you please, then pinning unpressed pleats or gathers at the jacket bottom until it comes in to the same size. This lower band will be applied the same as the front bands.

I assure you, it took longer to ***write*** about this jacket than it took to ***construct*** it. The remarkable rectangle is quick and easy; the perfect place for that special fabric.

center back
cut on fold
Cut 2 layers, one may be lining fabric.
center front

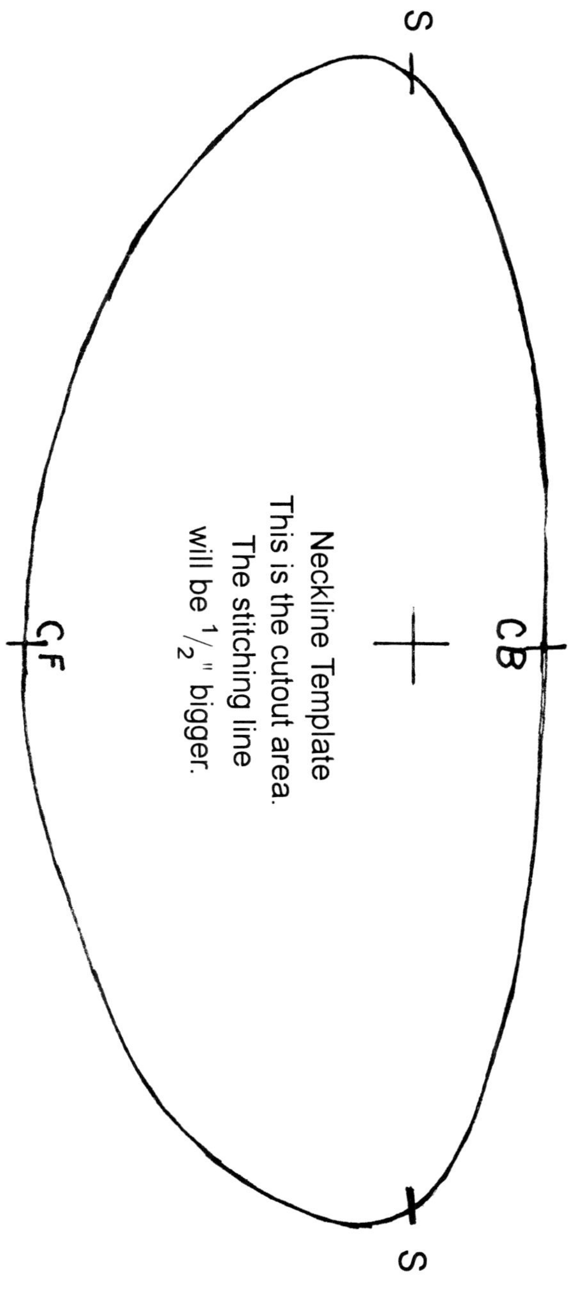
S
Neckline Template
This is the cutout area.
The stitching line
will be 1/2" bigger.
CB
CF
S

Stitch A Match

Program 12

We'll continue to develop ideas on a jacket introduced in program 11. A simple rectangle cut up the front collared, banded, folded and stitched together with added sleeves will complete it. While it's still flat, before any construction takes place, you may choose to lavishly embellish it. Go creative to make it uniquely yours.

Take a close look at the photo of Louise Mensing's jacket. From Virginia, she loaned this beautiful gray silk jacket. It is of gray silk noil painted faintly with a little pastel hinthere and there. The lining is gray charmeuse also painted or dyed with slight color splotches. The contrast of matte and shiny is lovely together; the similarity of color between the two fabrics is rich.

Let's consider what you might use for linings in a jacket. Don't just limit the choice to actual lining fabrics intended for that one use. Look elsewhere for a unique fabric to enrich the whole project.

For example, the lining in a black melton jacket (program 11) is a black and white print rayon. This little flash is interesting – and it came straight from my stash. I had some time ago purchased this fabric for a jacket. Deciding the print was too bold for my comfort, using it for a lining was the perfect solution.

Another print from my stash, a paisley print rayon challis, is the lining of a bronze leather jacket because the colors matched perfectly. Of course now that I've used it as a lining, what will I wear for the blouse?

The solid light blue washed rayon shown as a jacket in progress on this program is coupled with an Oriental pastel print cotton lining. What all these can do if they will be embellished is draw inspiration from the lining. The lining leads the way, hinting at ways you can embellish for a coordinated whole. Compare many fabrics and trims, and bring them into the grouping to try out for compatibility. If they don't quite comply, weed them out. With the remaining ones that seem to belong, let the lining dictate terms and you can stitch a match.

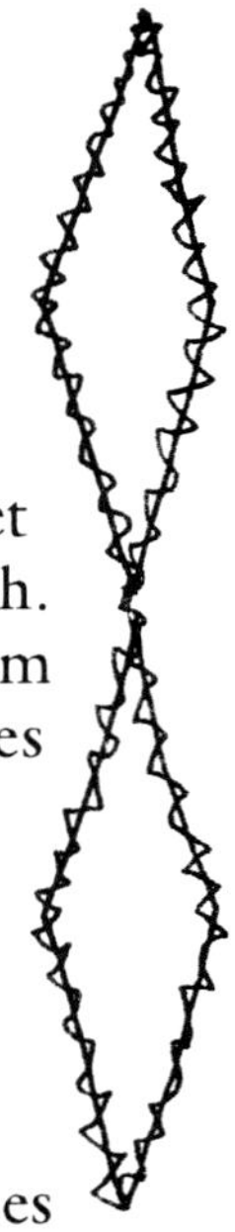

Designs on Louise's jacket are simple geometric shapes. Some diamond shapes are a taffeta whose crispness lends a contrast to the noil softness.

Cut a row of slashes in the jacket rectangle and weave self-fabric through. Secure the ends to keep them from pulling out, but leave the raw edges everywhere.

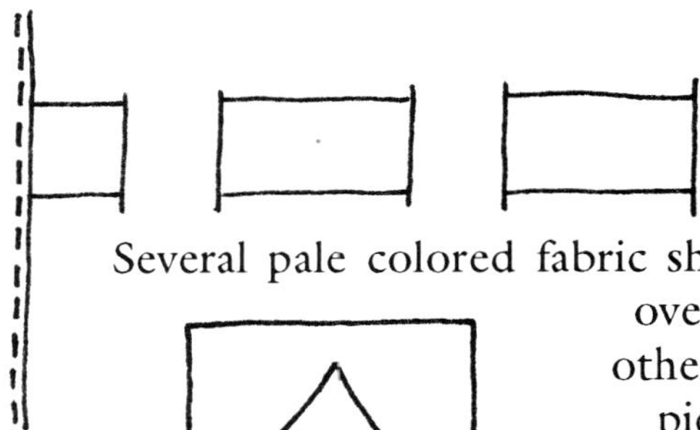

Several pale colored fabric shapes overlap each other, center-pieced by a little painted metal hinge. A small piece of stitched-on jewelry would be similar.

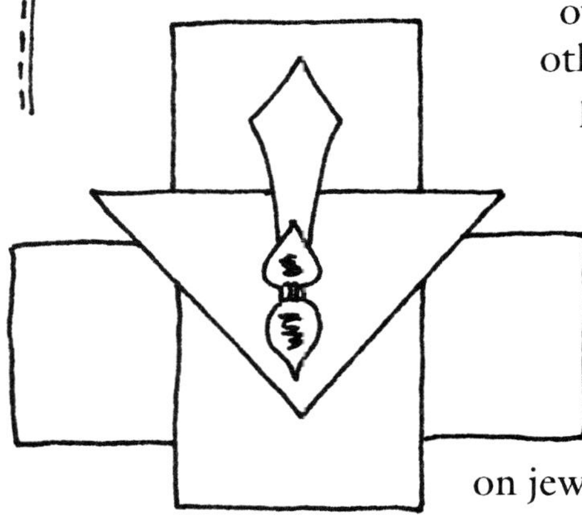

Part of her jacket front detail is why you would embellish when it is still a single layer rectangle, ***before*** it is slashed up the center front for an opening. The continuity of the horizontal and diagonal stripes is marvelous and effortless. Think how hard this could be if you tried to do it ***after*** the center front line was cut.

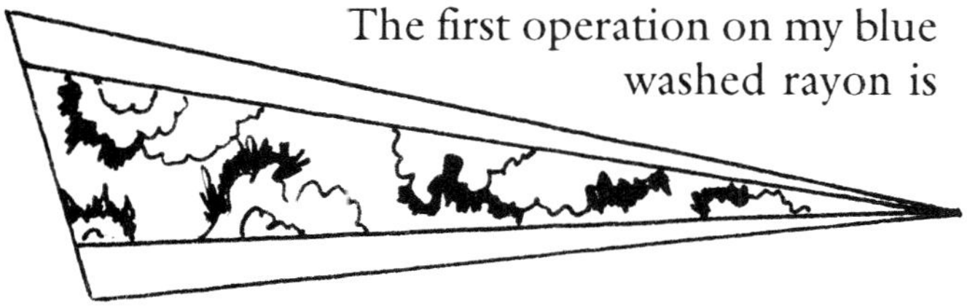

The first operation on my blue washed rayon is the triangular shaped slash pockets. Not only is the shape unusual, but the lips are more like bindings with an open space so the print pocket pieces can show. Slightly tricky, proceed like this:

Reinforce the backside where the pocket will be located with a patch of fusible interfacing cut 4" x 8" not only to protect edges from raveling, but also to support the additional pocket weight.

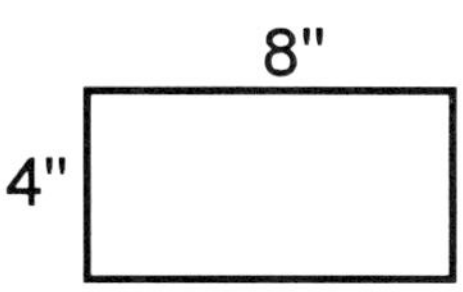

Choose a fabric for the two lip-bindings that can be self-fabric or a contrast. I used a lavender silk shantung, and cut it 2" longer and 3" wider than the finished space requires. Easier to work with when generous edges are provided, it can be trimmed down later if you like. On its backside draw the pocket shape. Position this

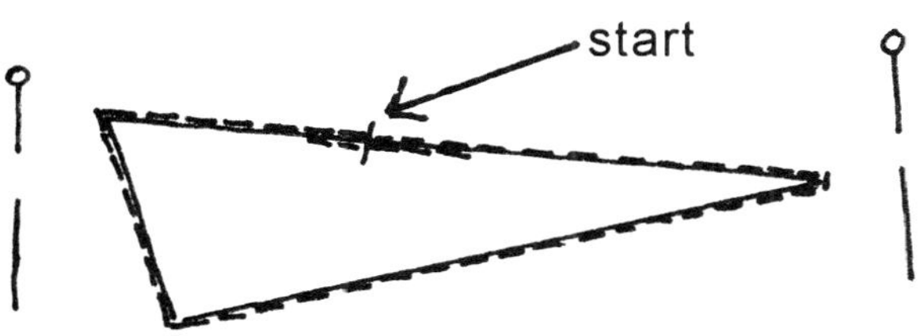

on the jacket front, right sides together, in the center of the interfaced area. Stitch exactly on your drawn line with small stitches to securely hold, especially at the sharp corners that will have very slim seam allowances. That sharpest corner might be softer if you stitch one extra stitch to slightly square it off and give it a tiny bit more fabric.

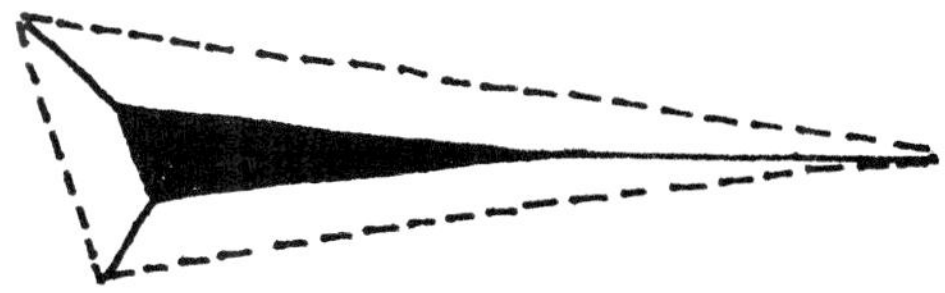

Start that stitching line not at a corner, but somewhere in the center. Overlap your stitches as you complete the stitching line. Partially cut out the center with sharp little scissors. Leave a scant 1/4" seam allowance all around, and discard the center.

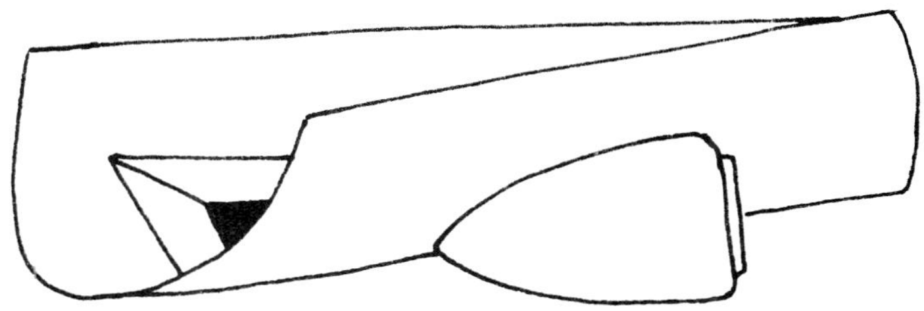

On each of the 3 sides, fold back the patch and press it flat, one at a time. Then pull the patch edges through the opening to the wrong side. Pull the short end over and press completely flat – **X**. Allow the two long

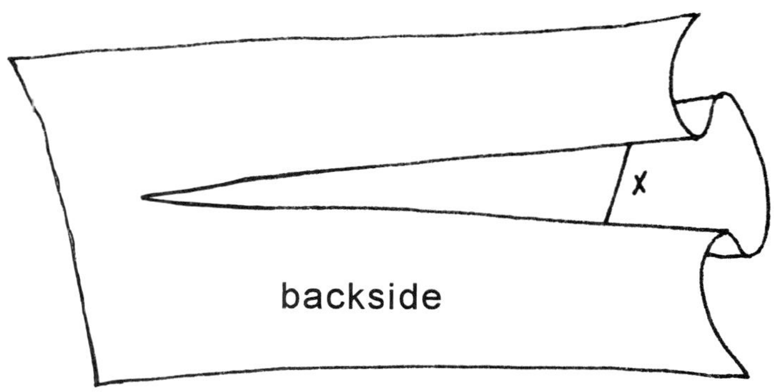

sides to relax and just be pressed back,

wrapping around the 1/4" seam allowance raw edges. Press flat with the end forming pleats. The front side will look like this.

Cut the pocket piece (I used the print lining) about 15" long and 4" wider than your finished pocket opening. This sounds very generous, but because of the odd stitching line angles, you'll be grateful for the excess.

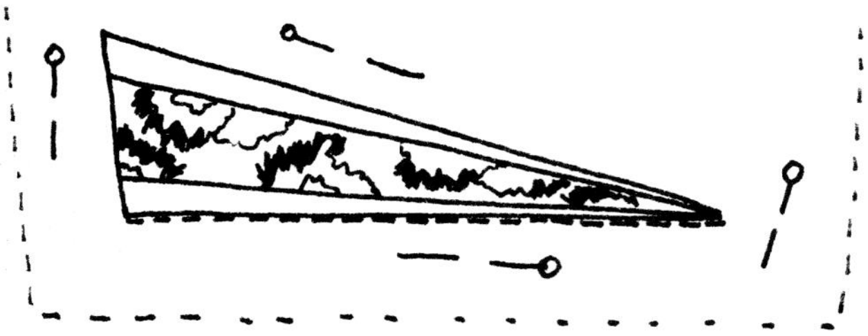

Attach this to the ***lower*** lip first. This is necessary to save yourself a lot of grief! Place right side of pocket against the wrong side of jacket as shown by the dotted lines that would be underneath, not showing. Stitch-in-the-ditch on the lower seam line to attach pocket piece to jacket.

On the jacket wrong side, press the pocket piece down where just stitched. Make a fold at the bottom, turning up so the upper edge almost covers the lip patch. Pin in place, pins out of the way of the next stitching line.

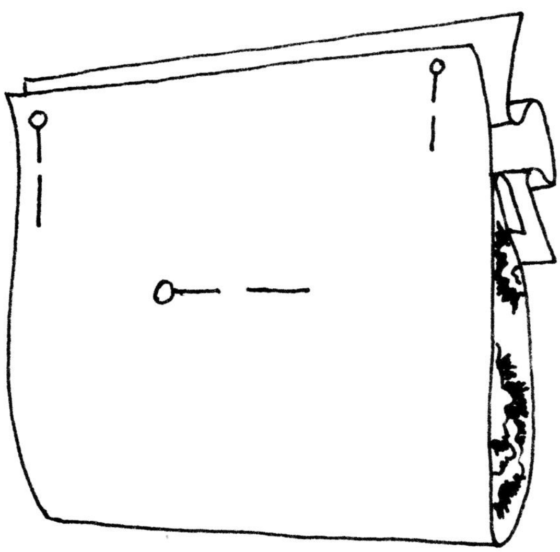

Again on the right side, ditch-stitch on the upper seam line. On the backside that newest stitching line will not be parallel with the pocket raw edge. This is as it should be.

All that remains is to complete the pocket from the right side. Turn back the

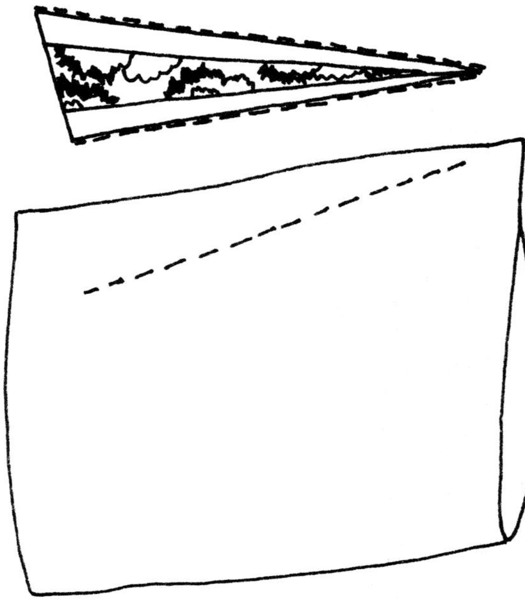

jacket right at the end. Sticking out flat on the table is the doubled-over pocket piece on the bottom, the pleated patch lips on top, and the jacket seam allowance uppermost. Stitch through all layers right next to the fold back. Repeat on the other pocket end. Press. This was an alternative to the program 11 patch pocket.

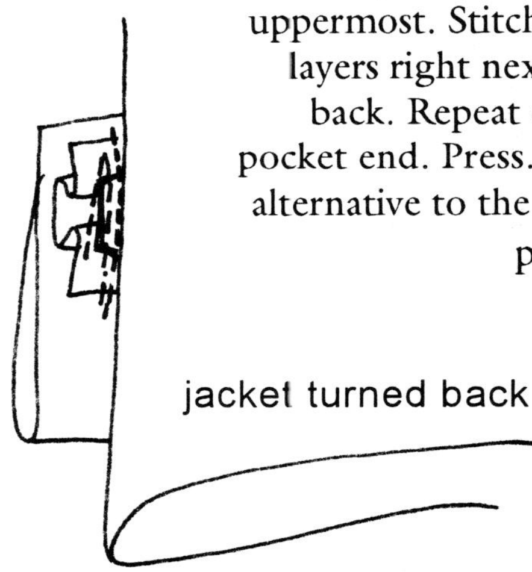

You're ready to add any adornments to the overall rectangle that please you. Once you've decided which fabric scraps will be used, press fusible sheets with peel-off paper to the back of each.

Cut many interesting shapes, and arrange them on your rectangle – be aware of the areas you might want to avoid. For example, there will be shoulder flanges stitched about midway. Except for some horizontal stripes that would look great when pleated up, other shapes you may not want to use as they would be concealed in the folds. Avoid the neckline as it will be cut out. I don't want to accent the bust so I'll take note of the approximate location.

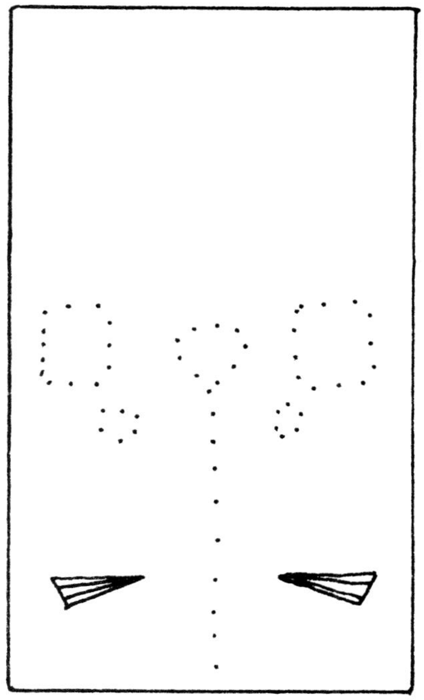

My Oriental print lining fabric has cherry blossoms on it. To appliqué them in their entirety may seem a little trite. They could be interesting cut in 2, partially obscured by an UltraSuede® squiggle.

A dimensional look, fold-edges left free, might work in places. First cut an elliptical shape in a fold of bias fabric. On the ironing board press it so that the cut edges form a straight line as you curve the fold. Slip those raw edges under the suede squiggle also.

Play with these pieces moving them around on the rectangle until you are happy with the results. Peel off the paper backing of each, fuse them down to the background. To stitch them down the monofilament nylon thread might be a good choice since it is invisible. Any potentially ravelly fabric will need to have a zigzag stitch over the edge. Suedes or leathers may be straight stitched. You can add many pieces but if the colors and values are similar to keep it muted, it will look rich rather than overdone. When finished, go back to program 11 directions to complete the construction of this jacket.

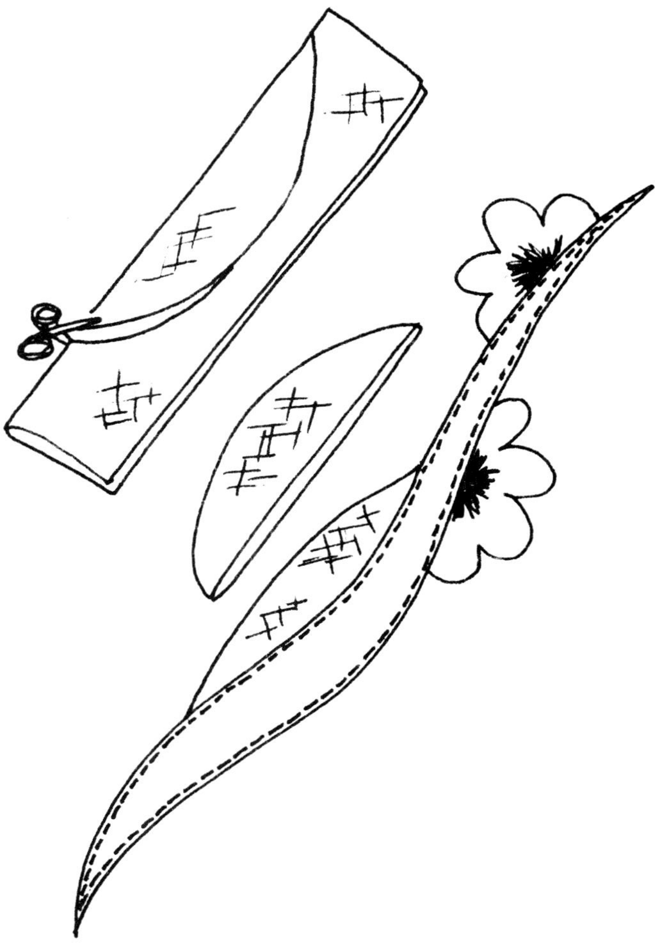

It's amazing how so many consider themselves untalented until they try some process such as this. Give it a try, and you can come up with something very attractive.

Strip With A Zip Program 13

Design your garment for multi-purpose usage. This jacket is a continuation of the simple rectangular-based jacket of the last two programs: design the sleeves to zip out, and convert that remarkable rectangle to a vest. A fur vest might be great over a heavy sweater and ski pants. Maybe alternate in that vest the fur sleeves with leather or with wool. Louise Mensing's silk jacket – when the day gets too warm, just zip the sleeves out and feel comfortable.

Let's look at the zippers that would make this possible. Coats and Clark® have a huge variety of separating zippers in all types, lengths, colors. Those you'd probably want to zero in on are the heavier molded teeth type, and the lighter weight coil type as well as medium weight metal. Lengths come in 2" increments from 12" to 24" in ten or so different colors. If your local store doesn't carry them, Call Coats and Clark® (number in the front of the book). They can help you get connected with whatever you need.

For a zip-in sleeve, insert the zipper ***before*** the coat side seams are sewn together, while the rectangle is still flat.

There's only one way a separating zipper can go in the sleeve. It will have to go in the sleeve. You'll not want the side that holds the slide dangling in the jacket armscye when the sleeve is zipped out. This sketch shows the position. The sleeves will be identical and interchangeable – no worry about which is left or right. Put the zipper in first and finish up the sleeve. There will be no confusion later about how the other zipper side goes in.

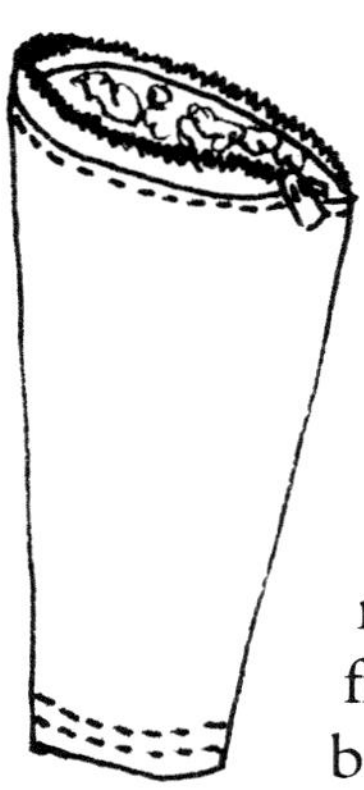

Start by locating the centers of every involved edge and marking. That means fold each zipper strip, and put a pin in its center. Fold the fashion fabric as well as the lining sleeve and clip each at the fold. Fold the jacket rectangle to find the exact midpoint that marks the shoulder. Pin crosswise or clip it also.

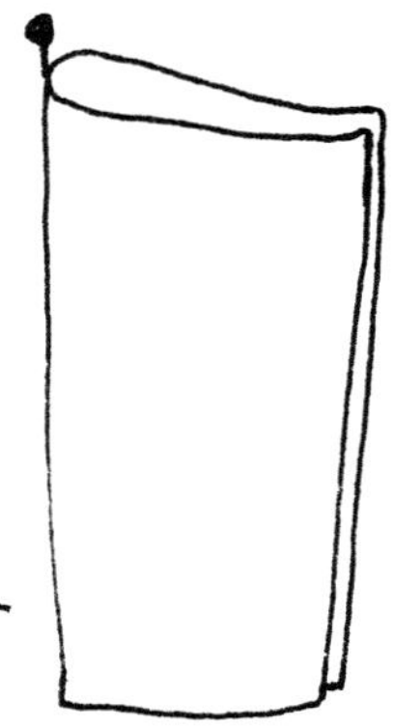

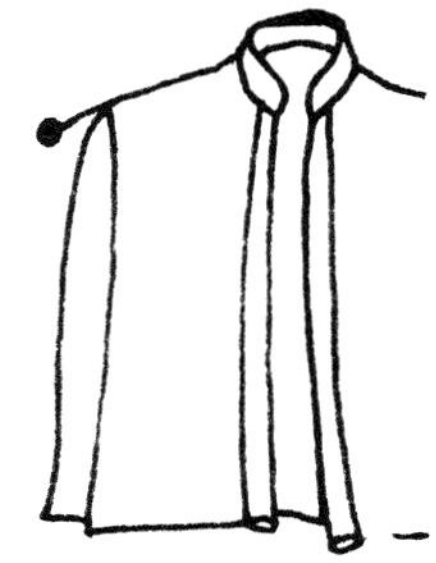

Stitch underarm seams of all sleeve pieces. Press open. The zipper right side is positioned on the fashion fabric right side – matching up the center points. The tape edge is even with the sleeve edge, teeth downward. These tapes are quite wide, and to stitch down its center is possible using a multipurpose presser foot. No zipper foot is needed since stitching close to the teeth is unnecessary. Large basting stitches will do.

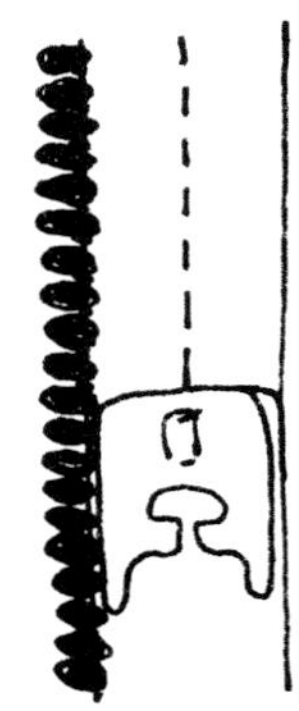

Right sides together, join lining sleeve over this, and with zipper between the two layers, retrace that original basting line. Do this in one operation if you're confident about teeth/foot edge position.

Turn sleeve right side out so that the teeth emerge and all raw edges are enclosed

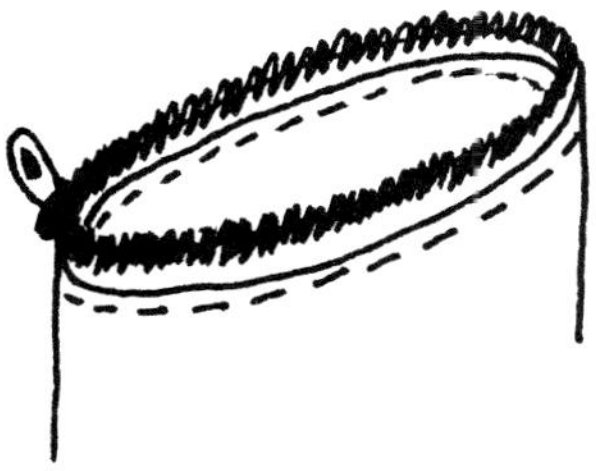

between sleeve layers. Finger press those folds flat then topstitch through all layers close to the fold edge. Move the needle position a little right or left to position it just as you want. This topstitching isn't mandatory, but it safely keeps the fabric away from the teeth.

This is not quite the same order in which it is demonstrated on the TV program. However this is the better way if you are unsure of the wrist length at this point. Save it until you can zip the sleeve in the finished jacket before you stitch in the hem to be sure it is as you like it.

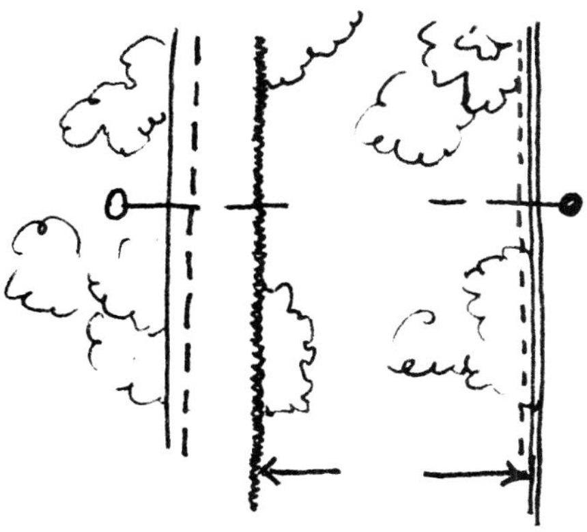

The jacket armscye is still flat, side seam not yet stitched. Position the zipper right side against the lining side of the jacket, matching the center markings. The zipper teeth should be 2" away from the fabric edge. Pin or baste in place, then machine stitch near the edge of the tape. This done on each armscye will mean that in the jacket left side it will begin zipping at the back, the slide ending up at the front. The right sleeve will zip in beginning at the front and end up in back.

In the faux leather shown on TV, the zipper had been basted in with two rows of hand basting so nothing would move and it would end up just perfect. If you do this, use silk or rayon fine thread so no impressions show. Ordinarily pinning is sufficient. Other precautions with the faux leather are putting strips of tissue under the stitching line if the leather side will be down on the machine bed. This allows easy movement without "dragging" on the metal of the machine. If the leather is on top, a teflon foot will work. Use the handly point-turner tool. Lay it on the leather, exerting only slight hand pressure. The teflon foot pushes it along in front. The tool does not permit the leather to scoot. Another leather tip is to sew with the lining side on top (non-stretchy), and the leather (stretchy knit backing) side on the bottom if the two are being sewn together. Experiment to see what works best for you. Finish the as instructed in program 11.

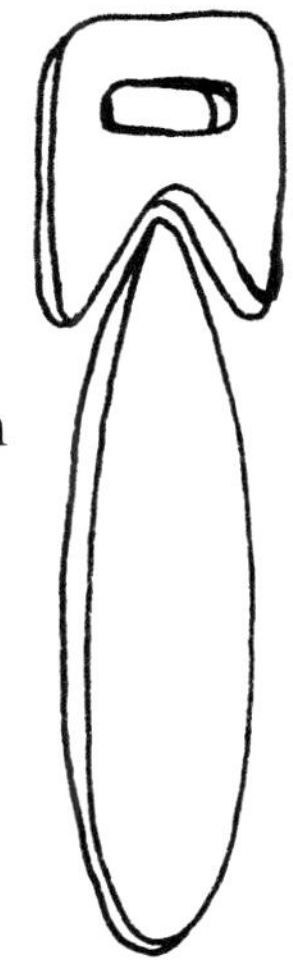

Another convertible project for this separating zipper is a skirt that can be short or long by zipping off a lower tier. Not for the A-line skirt though. The extra layers together with the zipper would be heavy and awkward, making it move like a hoop skirt when you move. Use on a slim skirt with the lightest weight separating zipper.

Because there is probably not a zipper long enough to go all the way around, use two zippers; one starting right next to where the next one ends. If the two together are too long for the width of the skirt, shorten and cut off. ***Where*** it is shortened is crucial. Cut off the end that does not affect the slide beginning. The zipper area where the shortening will occur ***must be unzipped*** because it must separate. Therefore, bartack each coil separately rather than together as would be stitched on most zippers.

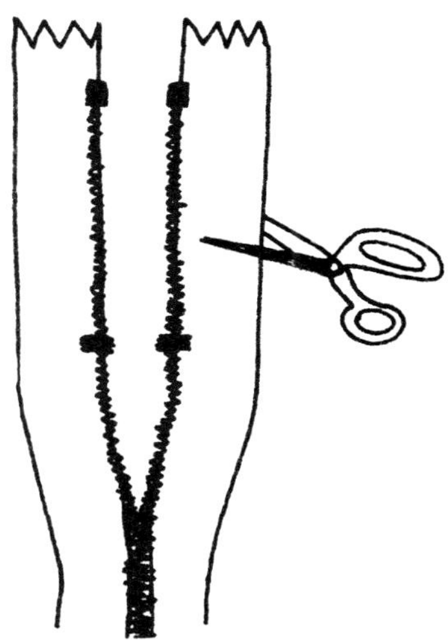

Just like the sleeve, **the lower skirt section is where the slide half of the zipper must be located** rather than having it dangle on the upper skirt when separated.

Machine baste the zippers to the top edge of the skirt extension, right sides together. Cover that with the lining, right sides together. Stitch all the way around except a 6" space left open at one end. Trim off the four corners. Turn the extension right side out and press all edges. Topstitch all around. This could also be left unlined according to personal preference.

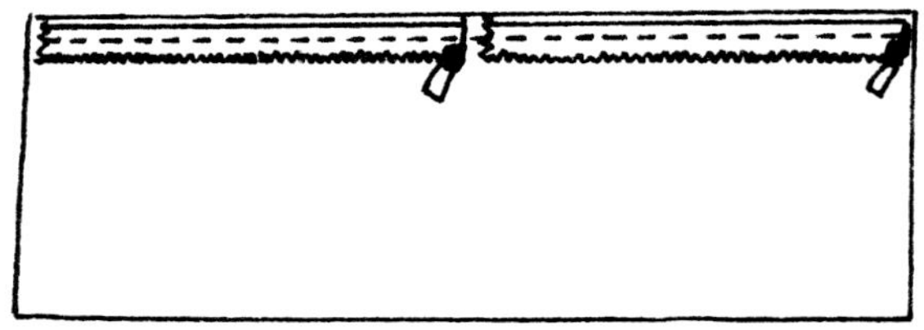

On the lower edge of the original skirt, right sides together, point the remaining two zipper halves. Locate the start and stop in the same position as the lower zipper halves. In the sketch, the slit is located in the front, but so long as both zippers are the same length it can be zipped on either back or front. Machine baste. Turn up the lower edge $1^{1}/_{4}$" to the inside. Pin in place. Topstitch 1" from the fold. When the lining is folded under against the zipper tape edge, either hand stitch or anchor with a second row of topstitching.

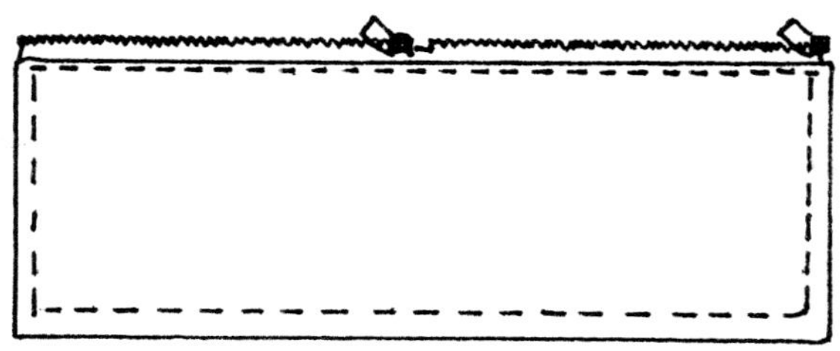

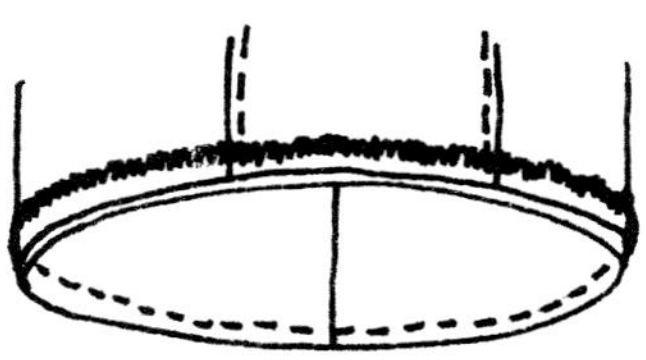

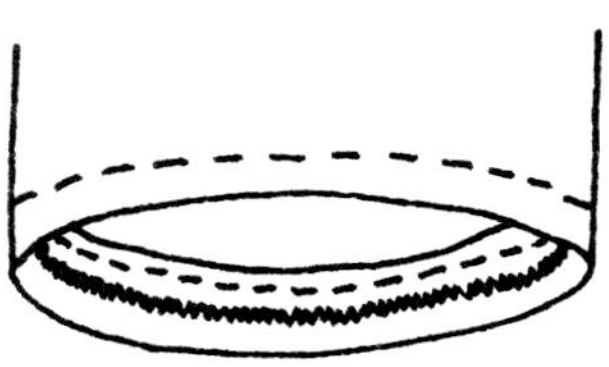

That was fun. Don't you just love to sew? Look around at what others wear or what is shown in shops, magazines, on TV or in movies. Keep remembering you can have anything you want when you sew because you really can do it yourself.

This was the last program in series 11 and where am I headed? On a busman's holiday of course, back to my sewing room. It's always a great adventure to go create, to discover new techniques, to see if I can't do better with each project.

What will series 12 involve? A lot of common sense as is the backbone of every series. Special techniques will be there using a machine to its fullest capabilities. Fabric manipulations for fun and serious fabric handling for very professional results. I'll produce a lot of new garments and I'll show many on loan from creative people around the nation. We'll do some nitty-gritty procedures along the way and all of it will be tied up with gorgeous ribbons. Come join the fun!